THE
FINGERPRINT
OF THE
ENTREPRENEUR

THE FINGERPRINT OF THE ENTREPRENEUR

Revised Edition

By:

Edward J. Fasiska, Ph.D.
and
Deborah Gay Fasiska

Laserlight Publishing
San Diego, CA

Acknowledgments

We would like to express our sincere appreciation and deepest thanks to the following people for providing us guidance, intellectual stimulation, and support while writing this book:

Our warm gratitude is extended to our mothers, Mary and Gertrude, and our fathers, John and Edward, for teaching and instructing us in many practical and philosophical areas of life. The resulting knowledge from these activities is one of our most cherished assets. We also hope, that in some way, this book will influence our daughter Desa's life in a positive manner and Ed's brother, John Fasiska Jr., with his goal to change his life.

We also would like to express our thanks to the following people for technical input and stimulating discussions resulting in many of the philosophies presented: Barbara Fasiska, Esq., Evelyn Fisher, Ph.D., Robert M. Fisher, Ph.D., Timmie A. Pollock, Ph.D., Lawrence J. Kashar, Ph.D., Jack Raley, Richard Weiss, Joe Wolzansky and especially Chuck Setler;

for editing: Mel Bernstein, Ph.D., Ed Dobransky Jr., Nancy Flohr, Marge Nasta, Ph.D., Melissa Padgett, Barbara Setler and especially Bess Carleton;

for collaboration with the Entrepreneurial Aptitude Test: Robert L. Durkin and Victor K. Kiam;

for the manuscript layout: Roy Aaron, Patti Bosco, Paul Bosco, David L. Hamilton, Gabe Marsico, Mary Parker and Norm Parker;

for much of the creative artwork: Tom Betush;

and for the cover photography, Sam Kresch.

Contents

Preface

"The Fingerprint of the Entrepreneur"

"The Fingerprint of the Entrepreneur" is an enlightening book that will enable you to change your life drastically. It cuts through the mystic of entrepreneurship, explicitly showing you what's involved, what's required, and how to become one. Focusing on a unique model of life, it outlines the necessary elements to change your life and elucidates a detailed path to achieve them. It also deals with the elements of success in general. The most appealing aspect of this book is that it not only discusses entrepreneurship, of more significance, it puts it within reach of the average aspiring business person.

In no uncertain terms, life-changing processes are complex. This is basically the reason that many people never change their lives significantly. That change they would like to make, but never do, may be starting their own business. This is primarily why the "Fingerprint of the Entrepreneur" was written, to enlighten and make the reader aware of this life-controlling reasoning, thus enabling you to take advantage of it. It should also be stated that "pure" aggressive behavior is not a substitute for the know-how, skills and resources needed to change your life or start a business.

One key to the potency of this book lies in the description of the personality and operational **"finger print"** of the *classic successful entrepreneur*. Also, the unique "Entrepreneurial Aptitude Test" measures your personal entrepreneurial profile. By comparing the two, your strengths and weaknesses in the business arena become apparent. A number of entrepreneurial tests have appeared in the literature. Others deal only with the effects or symptoms of entrepreneurship - not the cause or make-up of the entrepreneur. The Entrepreneurial Aptitude Test measures the fundamental elements of the reader that contribute to his or her entrepreneurial capability. Conversely, other tests to date measure only the symptoms of entrepreneurship such as risk-taking, yearn for autonomy, etc. They do not measure the inherent entrepreneurial character of the reader as does this test.

This book was written by a scientist/entrepreneur and a publisher/artist/entrepreneur and was based on data compiled while working with many entrepreneurs in various settings in a wide variety of business ventures. This work represents a sound analytical approach to an in-depth understanding and application of entrepreneurship. It does not deal with a single concept, but rather explores several facets of achievement, human behavior, and their role in life-changing processes.

Many people throughout the world are searching for some meaningful direction in their lives. *This book will help you to understand yourself better, thus helping you to find that new direction in your life.* Even more significant, it will help you to make the necessary changes to move forward into an enterprising venture; perhaps to work for yourself.

Introduction - Entrepreneurship and You

The Timing is Right -- The stage is set for your success in business.

We have experienced a time of extreme change. It was inevitable. The United States has shifted from a heavily industrialized to a *"high technology"* nation - an informational society. Many craftsmen and skilled laborers have been replaced by computers and technicians. Robotics is no longer a science-fiction term, but has become a reality. Students have personal computers which are slowly but surely replacing teachers.

This renaissance has created many new markets and the related potential to start new companies, especially small businesses. The entrepreneurial spirit in the United States is stronger than ever. Entrepreneurship has become the new *American dream*, especially with young people. The timing for this book is appropriate. Survival in this dynamic state-of-affairs requires adapting - changing one's life. "The Fingerprint of the Entrepreneur" was written to help entrepreneurs to be more effective, and to provide guidance and help to individuals moving forward in a new direction: by starting their own companies.

The first step in becoming an entrepreneur is to understand what an entrepreneur is, to determine the typical behavioral make-up of the entrepreneur. Having a psychological **"fingerprint"** of the *classic entrepreneur* gives us a goal, a reference profile to use as a role model.

*"The setting of goals and a positive attitude are not enough. Most of us, even the least successful, have goals and aspirations and want to: **reach for the stars.**"*

"The Fingerprint of the Entrepreneur" will not only describe in psychological terms the *classic entrepreneur* and his or her style of operation, but will measure your personal entrepreneurial profile as well. This will permit you to compare systematically your personality traits with those of the "entrepreneur", thus permitting you to identify your strengths and weaknesses in the entrepreneurial arena.

"The Fingerprint of the Entrepreneur" was also written to enable you to understand more realistically the mechanism of success in any endeavor, not only starting a business. The setting of goals and a positive attitude are not enough. Most of us, even the least successful, have goals and aspirations and want to *"reach for the stars"*. Just as wanting to build a house is not enough, you need resources and know-how in order to build it. The setting of goals or wanting to be successful in business is not enough; you must have resources to do this as well, and you have to **know how** to become successful.

Goals do play an important role in the success process though. There are two separate issues regarding goals. The first is the setting of them, and the second is the focusing on them and accomplishing them. This book deals more with the focusing on and accomplishment of goals. In fact, it is in this area that most successful people have the edge. Further, there is not necessarily a strong correlation between innate abilities and achieving goals or finding success. Goal setting and positive thinking deal with the current state-of-affairs (where we are now) and the desired result (where we want to go, i.e., starting a business, success). They do not, however, effectively answer the question of how to get there; for example, the mechanism of successfully starting your business. *This book provides that "missing link". That is, it bridges the gap between wanting to start your business and actually taking action to start it. It outlines what is necessary for your entrepreneurial success, evaluates your personal success traits, and suggests how you can change your life with this information.*

10

Finding success however, implies having your own definition of success. How we achieve success is related to how we perceive success. For many of us, only a part of our success formula is starting a business. It is important to realize that starting your business can be done in exactly the same manner as finding success in any other endeavor.

Success requires a personal definition. Success means different things to different people. There are as many kinds of successes as there are types of people. Success is related more to personal satisfaction than it is to any absolute measure. There may be success in your personal life, success in your career, success in your new business venture. Your personal formula for success is defined by the emphasis you place on these and on other areas in which you strive to be successful. For the entrepreneurial spirit however, a strong element in his or her success equation is working for himself or herself - autonomy is of paramount importance to the entrepreneur. For most individuals though, success is a unique combination or blend of all of these.

Success is elusive. The way we define success changes as we go through life. Our aspirations change. For example, in our younger years, we may think of success as having a good job or making a reasonable wage. Once we attain that goal, we realize that these do not provide the satisfaction that we thought they would and we change our minds about success. We may then redefine success as the accumulation of assets, for example, a home, a nice automobile, a pool in the backyard, etc. When we reach that point, we might again redefine success as having more leisure time in which to enjoy these assets. Usually, one of the final stages of success is recognition by our peers and perhaps even by the general public. *Success is elusive.* As we go through life, we reformulate our personal definition of success such that it reflects our slowly but steadily changing value system. We are always pushing ahead with a new definition of success, attempting to achieve new goals. This will be the case in your new entrepreneurial venture as well. As it

11

*"**Success is elusive.** As we go through life, we reformulate our personal definition of success such that it reflects our slowly but steadily changing value system."*

develops, your criteria for judging the success of your entrepreneurial venture will change also.

How do we arrive at our personal formula for success - that unique blend of personal success, business success, success in our careers, having power, money, etc? The answer to this question is important since it represents the source of all of our motivation. **Our unique formula for personal success is determined by our value system.** We define success by what we value and likewise, we are motivated to achieve only what we value. Although usually done subconsciously, we tend to equate success with items high on our list of priorities, those stemming from our value systems. Most of you reading this book value starting your own business and, therefore, this fits into your success equation. Simply stated, your value system represents what you really want in life. Consequently, it also represents the source of your motivation. Understanding this enables you to focus more clearly on what you really want to do and then ultimately, to do it. The point of this logic is to encourage you to do some *soul-searching* - to decide what you really want in life. If you really want your own business, you can have it. Your value system will provide the motivation and the knowledge in this book will provide the know-how and guidance.

The research for this book consisted of observing the styles of operation, interviewing and working with many entrepreneurs who had founded and were running their own companies. In many instances, we worked directly with them acting as an advisor to their research programs to help develop new products or systems for the marketplace. This working relationship provided an excellent environment to observe their operational traits and thinking patterns. Also, as part of the preparation for this book, many experts were interviewed to get their ideas and theories on success and entrepreneurship. They consisted of entrepreneurs and executives in business and industry and deans, department heads, and researchers in academia. Their ideas and thoughts, along with our research results, were woven into the basic theory of the personal sphere of equilibrium (PSE) and its model. This model coupled with the included psychological interpretation of entrepreneurship provides the basis for understanding and changing your entrepreneurial potential. It is this reasoning that can be so helpful in starting your own company. These concepts do not conflict with other theories based on ideas and philosophies such as goal setting, psychocybernetics, positive thinking, etc., but rather tends to complement, supplement, and in fact, unify them.

Before reading further, please turn to Appendix A and take the "Entrepreneurial Aptitude Test." Do not read further until you have taken the test.

If you do read further before taking the test, the results will be influenced. This will distort the description of your personal entrepreneurial profile emerging from the entrepreneurial aptitude test and dilute the guidance this book can provide in helping you to start your business.

Place your answers on the Entrepreneurial Aptitude Test Answer Sheet in Appendix A.

Do not attempt to grade or interpret the results at this point. They will be discussed later. You will receive detailed instructions later in the book to interpret your test results.

If you are interested in a more in-depth and comprehensive evaluation of your test which focuses on your personal entrepreneurial profile, including suggestions that will help you in your entrepreneurial endeavors, do the following:

Send your original answer sheet (make a copy of it first for your own use) with $4.95 for processing, evaluation, tax and postage to:

Laserlight Publishing
Suite 104-337
6992 El Camino Real
Rancho La Costa, CA 92009

> **en•tre•pre•neur** \ *n : one who organizes, manages, and assumes the risk of a business or enterprise.*

CHAPTER I

Your Personal Sphere of Equilibrium

Please bear with us. The first two chapters or this book, but only the first two, are a bit technical. We felt as though this background was <u>necessary</u> to show the reader the sound basis of the concepts presented - they didn't come out of thin air. The remainder of the chapters are *lighter*, dealing more with how these concepts can be applied in <u>your</u> life.

"The Fingerprint of the Entrepreneur" is based on sound logic and facts with very little assumption. Conclusions that we will use later regarding entrepreneurial concepts are drawn through deductive reasoning. Throughout this book we will introduce some simple scientific principles to demonstrate the universal nature of the concepts that are presented. Scientific principles are simply laws of nature. Keep in mind that the validity of many arguments or ideas are established very easily: Do they always hold true? Scientific principles always do!

This chapter will explain a unique model of life devised specifically for this book and based on scientific principles. Remember, scientific principles are universal and therefore hold true for all applications. This model applies to our everyday life and our ability to interact effectively with the outside world both personally and in our business ventures. Also, by referencing your results from the Entrepreneurial Aptitude Test, you will gain insight about yourself in the business arena. To begin, we will first discuss the principle of

16

equilibrium and how it pertains to our model of life.

Equilibrium is a principle of nature. Most of us live in a state of equilibrium. That is to say, we live in a relatively unchanging state. This state represents an equilibrium between the day-to-day activities of our lives and the rest of the world. In this state of equilibrium, we have relatively fixed responsibilities to ourselves, families, employers, and to society in general. We have relatively fixed activities, incomes, friends, and contacts. Our lives just don't change much from day to day. Further, although we usually don't think of it quite this way, we must exert energy to maintain that equilibrium. For example, if we have a regular 9 to 5 job, five days a week, we know that we have to report to that job or we may lose it, thus upsetting our equilibrium. If we do not perform well at our job and get fired, this would have a detrimental effect on our life. By the same token, if we don't honor our other responsibilities to our families and friends (and these may be subtle responsibilities) our lives may also change, probably for the worse.

We as human beings are concerned with the basic needs of existence and security: food, shelter, etc. We have other needs as well: emotional needs, social needs, cultural needs, etc., but these are secondary, only being sought after our basic needs are satisfied. Because our needs are satisfied in our equilibrium state, we are willing to expend energy to sustain our natural equilibrium. We do this because we subconsciously associate our equilibrium condition *(our life as we live it)* with fundamental security. This equilibrium sphere of friends, acquaintances, contacts, activities, events and needs that surround each of us, we will call our **Personal Sphere of Equilibrium (PSE).**

In a sense, we may define this personal sphere of equilibrium as the **comfort zone,** in which we operate in our day-to-day lives. This sphere contains many elements of our personal life: friends, jobs, careers, responsibilities, and, in fact everything else that we are personally involved with.

*"In a sense, we may define this personal sphere of equilibrium as the **comfort zone**, in which we operate in our day-to-day lives. This sphere contains many elements of our personal life: friends, jobs, careers, responsibilities, and, in fact everything else that we are personally involved with."*

18

In fact, over 99% of our lives is spent within our PSE. This sphere is dynamic. It is constantly developing, ever so slowly, as we move through life. Its development began in childhood and has been continuing ever since. In fact, our sphere will continue to change as long as we are on this earth. The personal sphere of equilibrium concept can be understood from two points of view. The first is a philosophical one, and the second is a scientific interpretation of the philosophical approach. Let's begin with a philosophical explanation of how our spheres or personal domains developed.

Our personal spheres of equilibrium exist as a natural result of the exposure and events that we have encountered during and since our childhood. Some of our contacts and experiences have had very profound effects in molding our sphere; others have had moderate effects; still others have had no effect at all. This complex array of exposure to people, events, and experiences has molded our personal domain into what it is today.

Throughout the years, we have constantly experienced an influx of ideas, information, and events from our external environment into our sphere. For a variety of reasons, much too detailed and complex for us to understand completely, some of the information has been retained in our sphere and some has been rejected. Therefore, the aggregate of information and experience that has been retained now represents the contents of your personal sphere. In one way, your sphere is a complex record, a fingerprint of your experiences, which has been tempered by your natural traits. In another way, it represents the total of the resources that you have at your disposal to accomplish something - for example, starting your own business. Your sphere may or may not have entrepreneurial traits in it. You'll find out when we discuss your Entrepreneurial Aptitude Test (or E Q Test) results.

The parallel discussion of your sphere involves the very fundamental principle of nature, that of equilibrium. Remember, a test of the validity of a concept is its universal applicability and it is remarkable how well the principle of equilibrium applies to this model of your life. Equilibrium, in a scientific sense, implies an isolated physical system (a place set apart from the rest of the world). Consider this -- your life is also an isolated system. *You don't really live in the world at large -- more accurately -- you live in your personal domain, which is essentially isolated from the world.*

The general law of equilibrium is: *an isolated system will eventually gravitate toward an equilibrium condition unless it is acted upon by external forces.* In other words, the system will automatically reach equilibrium (a steady-state condition where no further change occurs). There are many examples of this phenomenon around us. To demonstrate the idea, let's look at one: If we drop several ice cubes into a glass of water, the system will naturally tend toward equilibrium. In other words, the water will become colder and the ice will become warmer and begin to melt. Eventually, the ice melts and after some time, the system will reach a temperature at which the water is in equilibrium with its surroundings. This will happen naturally. That is, the water will spontaneously reach room temperature - after that there will be no further tendency for the liquid to change temperature; the system has found its equilibrium. From that point on, unless the system is acted upon by some external force, for example, another ice cube is dropped into the water, its temperature will remain the same.

The scientific principle of equilibrium, demonstrated by the example of ice and water, also applies to the personal sphere of equilibrium model of our lives. As we said before, our sphere represents an equilibrium between our everyday lives and the world. Both the ice water and our personal sphere of equilibrium sphere are isolated systems. Both systems are subject to and will behave according to the well established scientific principle of equilibrium.

Exactly in the same manner that the liquid equilibrium could be changed by external forces, that is, dropping in an ice cube, the equilibrium between our sphere, our lives and its environment, can also be changed by external forces. ___Your life is not easily changed from within.___ Some sort of an "ice cube" (**external stimulus**) must be dropped into it from outside your sphere to precipitate change.

In most cases, external information (experiences, events, ideas) is constantly entering our spheres and tends to broaden them slowly. The amount of new exposure that we have controls the rate of broadening of our personal sphere of equilibrium. The quality of our new experiences affects the enrichment of our sphere. As is typical for most equilibria, although there is a constant influx of information, ideas, and events into our lives, there is also a constant rejection of ideas, information, and events. In the final analysis, the integral of the data that is taken in and not rejected on a day-to-day basis ultimately determines the depth and quality of our sphere.

There is a vast amount of information within our personal spheres that took years to accumulate. Therefore, the current daily or weekly filtering of relatively small amounts of new information into the sphere results in only minor changes. In other words, it is difficult to induce rapid change in a system, our PSE (our life), that took years and years to create. To change our spheres (our lives) drastically requires the action of external forces. The implication of this is: *significantly changing your life requires an externally oriented approach.* This applies to starting your business as well. You need an externally oriented approach (to play the role of the *ice cube*) to start your business. Examples of external forces are: a new partner, an external advisor, an external investor, etc.

The world is filled with many equilibria. In fact, equilibria are what tend to keep the status quo (keeps the world in order). There are all sorts of equilibria. Even in our bodies, for example, biological equilibria keep our body chemistry in order. If it were not for equilibria tending to keep order, the world would be chaos. We should realize, though, that the term equilibrium does not imply unchanging. The world is changing but usually slowly and predictably and almost imperceptibly - our spheres are also changing in the same slow controlled fashion.

There was a tremendous amount of philosophy involved in the molding of our spheres. However, we are not primarily interested in how our spheres formed. Instead, we are more interested in understanding our sphere, its breadth, qualities and weaknesses. We are also interested in using its contents to help to change our lives, perhaps to start a business.

Our personal domains began to form when we were infants and have been developing ever since, in a manner that was acceptable to us, a manner that would produce a sphere that we would be willing to live in, a comfort zone. Most of us, throughout the years, have developed skills in specific areas. Usually the entrepreneurial skills are surprisingly rare. Most of us were not taught to be entrepreneurs -- we have yet to learn and become comfortable with entrepreneurial skills. As we will see later, some of us, because of our backgrounds and our psychological traits, will be more adept at learning the entrepreneurial skills than others.

We live in this sphere that is in equilibrium with our environment, **we do not interact with the world.** Our sphere is insulated from the world. Therefore, each day of our lives is fairly similar. We really live in or operate in our personal sphere. We are in equilibrium with the world, but **we live in our sphere.** The isolated system of your life is in equilibrium with the world around you. Do you have any doubts about that? Have you ever realized how difficult it is to change your life significantly? Inducing change in your life is identical to changing any other isolated system. Therefore, if you do not have the resources to initiate your entrepreneurial activities in your sphere, you had better look elsewhere. Remember, you need an *external force* to help you change direction in your life. This book will show you how to find it.

CHAPTER II

Success Waits Outside Your Sphere

The breadth, quality and diversity of the Personal Sphere of Equilibrium (PSE) varies from individual to individual - different spheres contain different contents. We're not all equal. For example, some of us have been exposed to entrepreneurial activities and some of us have not. To some degree the size of our sphere is a function of age. As we grow from child to teenager to young adult, the personal sphere of equilibrium generally increases. This increase is a result of our accumulated experience and learning in the forms of formal and informal education, and increased exposure to new ideas as well as the meeting of new people. It is not only our formal education and other structured learning that affect the breadth of the PSE, but it is also the guidance that we receive along the path of life. Many of us have been lucky enough to have had influential *gurus* or *mentors* whose guidance not only helped us broaden our spheres, but also to establish or modify our value systems.

Our cultural backgrounds also affect the content and breadth of our personal sphere of equilibrium. For example, it would be reasonable to assume that a child of a prominent diplomat would have a broader sphere than, for the sake of argument, the sphere of an underprivileged child. The diplomat's child would probably be exposed to more travel, culture and education. Very often, however, it is the subtle differences in our lives that become important. A small item of creative input at a timely receptive period might trigger a rapid expansion of the sphere in a new direction, resulting in new possibilities and a changed outlook - this is usually the manner in which the entrepreneurial element is introduced.

Success lies outside your sphere whether it be working for an employer or working for yourself. Unless you already consider yourself successful, the road to success lies outside your sphere. If we do not have success within our sphere, we must go outside our sphere to find it. The implication of this reasoning becomes apparent. As an example, a key to starting your own business is the willingness and the ability to emerge from your sphere and work outside of your sphere; these are the activities that can change your life. These are the external forces that can change your life, in the same way that the ice cube dropped in a glass of water can change that equilibrium. As we said before, most people feel secure within their sphere. It is, in a sense, their comfort zone. Conversely, they feel insecure outside their sphere; that is, they are uncomfortable working in areas that are unfamiliar to them. How does one become successful? In the answer to that question lies the underlying reason as to why some people find success easier than others. Successful people have the ability to move out of their sphere with some degree of ease. Part of the reason they can do this may have to do with their psychological make-up. We will discuss this in the next chapter. They are more likely, for example, to actually start their business, rather than just talk about it. At a very minimum, individuals who tend to be successful can move out of their spheres in spite of the discomfort which they experience. On the other hand, individuals who have difficulty finding success, usually find it difficult to move out of their spheres at all.

There is another related issue that should be considered as well. It should provide encouragement and motivation to work outside your sphere. This issue deals with the essence of how our lives evolve: The fate of our lives in the long run - our destiny - is decided in relatively short control time intervals,

"How does one become successful? In the answer to that question lies the underlying reason as to why some people find success easier than others. Successful people have the ability to **move out of their sphere** *with some degree of ease."*

at key periods in our lives. We have all experienced these decision points. Some examples of these are: to get married or to stay single, to get divorced or to stay unhappily married, to go to school or to take a job, to start your own business or to work for someone else, to move out of state or to live where you have lived your entire life, etc. Decision making time windows in our lives are relatively short, but they may influence our lives drastically and permanently. They, in a sense, help to determine the fate of our lives.

The important consequence of this reasoning is that we can determine the destiny of our lives by making decisions, working hard and spending energy in very short time intervals in our lives. **Successful lives are not necessarily a result of constant hard work;** rather, and in fact, they are usually a result of our making the right moves during key short control periods. Working in areas outside of our sphere, even for short time periods, is the secret to starting your business. Once you establish momentum and are on a course headed for success, that momentum is easier to maintain. The difficult step for most individuals is beginning, since this represents the initial excursion from the sphere.

I'm sure that you have all heard that *success is a result of being "goal oriented."* This is a fallacy. Most unsuccessful people are goal oriented as well. That is to say, unsuccessful people usually have well defined goals; they usually know exactly what they would like to do; they just don't do it. Talk to a vagrant on any street, he will tell you exactly what he would like to do. Being goal oriented merely identifies the target. It is a necessary, but not sufficient, prerequisite. What is needed as well, or maybe even more, is the mechanism to hit that target. Almost without question, in every instance, to start your business means to change your life, from the equilibrium situation you find yourself locked into at the current time (your sphere), by aiming yourself in a new entrepreneurial direction and moving in that direction. That is the crux of the issue. This logic applies to finding success in general and certainly to starting your own business. Wanting to start your business and setting goals are not enough. A plan of action, implemented outside of your sphere, is what will make it happen. Because of this, your natural resources that help you to move out of your sphere are important. These will be discussed later.

Again, we would like to introduce another fundamental, scientific principle as an aid to understanding the logic behind spending energy in unfamiliar areas to promote change in our lives. **"Activation energy"** is a common scientific phenomenon found in nature and one that controls many events. Probably one of the best ways to explain or understand the principle of activation energy is by example. Activation energy is found in many simple chemical reactions. Let's look at one: If we mix oxygen gas with hydrogen gas absolutely nothing will happen. The two gases will simply tolerate each other and coexist. However, if we ignite the mixture, a violent explosion occurs, releasing tremendous amounts of energy and forming a new product, water.

Hydrogen + Oxygen + (a spark) = Water + Energy

This is the reaction that takes place when using hydrogen as a fuel. The reaction between hydrogen and oxygen does not take place until some energy is supplied to the gas mixture. In this case the activation energy is the spark. The gas mixture at the point of the spark has the activation energy to enable the oxygen and hydrogen to combine rapidly to form water. The reaction will continue furiously until all of the gas mixture reacts, thus producing the explosion. The chemical reaction does not take place until its activation energy is supplied - the gas mixture then explodes violently. Many reactions and processes in nature require a little activation energy before they will occur. Another simple example of activation energy is the dislodging a large round rock from a hillside. After the initial effort (activation energy), a great amount of energy is released as the rock rolls down the hill.

Activation energy applies to how we get things done as well: To change our lives, our career paths, or perhaps to accomplish something that we always wanted to accomplish, we have to supply the activation energy first. This energy is often surprisingly small but is usually required outside of our sphere in areas that we are unfamiliar and uncomfortable with. However, as in the case of oxygen combining with hydrogen, after the activation energy is supplied, the reaction becomes self-perpetuating. This is also true for starting our own business; once we begin by working outside of our sphere, our business development will tend to become more spontaneous. Also keep in mind that the longer we work in an area outside of our sphere, the more comfortable it becomes to us and the easier it will be to do so. Perhaps it also becomes a little easier because our value system is modified a bit. Working in these short time periods provides the activation energy to initiate our entrepreneurial careers.

There are other variables, however, that play a role in becoming successful. There are variations in natural and acquired resources such as intelligence, formal education, experience, the ability to work hard, determination, motivation, positive attitude, etc. These resources must be used effectively. The first step in utilizing resources and attributes is the setting of goals. Remember that there is a big difference between the setting of goals and the accomplishing of goals. The accomplishment of a goal is related to the ability to focus on that goal and to carry it through to the end. Very often life-changing goals lie outside your sphere, and the individuals that typically accomplish these goals do so because they are willing to leave their spheres (break out of them).

The excursions from our sphere that we discussed so far have all been planned and intended to promote desired changes. However, from time to time, there are other excursions from our sphere that are unplanned and usually come at times of severe crisis. These should be mentioned to reinforce the idea of the universal application of the sphere model.

*"Very often life-changing goals lie outside your sphere, and the individuals that typically accomplish these goals do so because they are willing to leave their spheres (**break out of them**)."*

Since our sphere represents an equilibrium condition, we are constantly making adjustments to preserve that equilibrium. If the imbalances within an individual's sphere become extremely severe, for example, at a time of crisis, he may emerge from his sphere simply to protect it. In other words, just as we leave the sphere to induce change, to move forward into a new venture, there are times when we might have to leave our sphere, do things that we normally would not do to maintain the status-quo of our life. An example of this might be a mild-mannered individual who, if his safety or that of a member of his family is at stake, may, for an instant, leave his sphere and act in a manner completely foreign to him to protect the integrity of his sphere.

In other words, although we usually leave our sphere to enhance it, there may be times when we leave it simply to protect what is already there. In those incidents, the desire to move out of your sphere is directly proportional to how critical the situation is. If the situation is critical enough that it may have a traumatic effect on your life, then an excursion outside of your sphere is triggered automatically. Although success lies outside our sphere, from time to time we may also make excursions outside our sphere just to maintain that equilibrium which represents our fundamental security.

Yes - success does lie outside your sphere. This is particularly true when starting a new entrepreneurial venture. A plan of action must be implemented which includes *"breaking out"* of your sphere.

What are the factors that control your ability to work out of your sphere? Are these entrepreneurial skills that you can learn? The answers to these questions lie in the analysis of the "style-of-operation" of the entrepreneur and your entrepreneurial resources. We will say much about this. It should be mentioned at this point, however, that "pure" aggression is not the answer to changing your life -- it is more complex than that. Leaving your sphere implies a well-thought-out assertive action driven by a deep inner desire to change.

This is accompanied by a realistic evaluation of the necessary skills and resources needed to accomplish your objective.

Initially, a profitable exercise would be a realistic self-appraisal of your resources in your sphere. Attempt to ascertain what is included in your sphere. Take some time and do this - it will be a worthwhile exercise. A good way to proceed is to make a list or ponder all your resources: education, skills, talents, friends, contacts, finances, strengths, etc., that may help you in starting your business or other life-changing activity. This is not a trivial exercise. It represents a personal accounting of the resources at your disposal - don't overlook any. Are there any obvious gaps or weaknesses either in resources or personality traits? Analyze and get to know your _business-self_ or your resources that relate to other life changing activities that you may be contemplating. The Personal Sphere of Equilibrium Resource Outline in Appendix B will help you itemize your pertinent resources.

CHAPTER III

Personality Overtones

To this point we have focused on the concept of the Personal Sphere of Equilibrium (PSE), a model describing your personal isolated environment. In a sense your sphere represents the miniature limited world in which you exist. Your sphere is a snapshot, at any point in time, of everything in your life. Among other things, this environment contains the resources that can be used to accomplish your goals, for example, starting your own business. What we haven't discussed is the manner in which you operate in that sphere - how you use those resources.

As human beings we have our own distinctive temperaments and styles of operating. What is in your sphere is one thing, but how you use it is quite another. How you like to function, including using your resources, is largely determined by your personality type. Thus, everything we have discussed so far deals with defining our sphere and describing its contents. What I would like to do now is introduce the element of behavior into the personal sphere of equilibrium (PSE) concept.

In psychological-typing exams, a statement is often included in the instructions: "There are no right or wrong answers in this test. These answers only indicate the way you prefer to look at things." Well, this is probably true and the psychologists are most likely correct; however, the way you prefer to look at things is certainly likely to affect your ability to perform a task, achieve a goal, be successful, or start your business. It is for this reason that we are going to introduce and discuss some well accepted psychological concepts that shed light on the fundamental differences on the ways people think. This is of utmost importance to you since the way you prefer to function is the key to how you use or take advantage of the contents of your sphere.

Becoming successful is not a natural exercise, but achieving success, especially in business, as we will see in this chapter, is easier for some than for others depending on their attitudes and their personalities. We have to go out of our way to become successful. Stated otherwise, many activities involved with becoming successful lie outside our sphere.

People are different in fundamental ways. They have different desires, values, motives, aims, purposes, impulses, emotions, etc. They operate differently. They have different strengths and different weaknesses. They have different wants and different beliefs. In short, there are radical differences in people. Therefore, it is logical to assume that there are differences in the tendencies for various individuals to become successful or to begin a new business venture. For example, the entrepreneur desperately seeks autonomy, is intuitive, flexible, deals well with confusion, action-oriented, and has a yearning for risk - hardly average personality traits.

The following is a condensed version of the well known psychological-typing theory postulated by Swiss physician and psychologist, C. G. Jung. He developed one of the most comprehensive and widely accepted theories to explain human personality and differences in human behavior. Jung's theory of psychological type postulates that we have four basic mental functions, which he called *"sensing, intuition, thinking, and feeling"*. Everyone uses these mental processes but each of us *prefers* some processes over others and usually better develops the preferred processes. We each use all four processes but we are distinguished (classified) by our relative preferences for each and by the attitudes with which we use them. Jung essentially said that people are basically different, even though

*"**People are different** in fundamental ways. They have different desires, values, motives, aims, purposes, impulses, emotions, etc. They have different strengths and different weaknesses. They have different wants and different beliefs. In short, there are radical differences in people."*

they all have the same multitude of instincts to drive them from within. One instinct is no more important than another. What is important though, is our preference for how we like to function or how we think about things.

Isabel Myers formulated the Myers-Briggs Type Indicator. This was essentially a comprehensive psychological test based on Jung's original work and was intended to put Jung's theory into practice. There are other recognized psychological testing exams as well, but the Myers-Briggs is considered to be one of the best available. The results of type indicator tests now have global applications. A few typical examples are: to determine how people will get along, how people will complement each other, or to point out likely sources of misunderstanding between different types of individuals. They are even used to recommend careers or to pair up roommates. It seems logical to assume that a modified and expanded psychological typing exam, such as the one developed for this book, which tests for entrepreneurial traits as well, can be a useful tool to help indicate one's tendency for entrepreneurship - assuming we know the necessary personality and operational elements of entrepreneurship.

The following is a condensation of the four pairs of preferences, used to distinguish personalities and which represent the substance of the psychological typing concept. This explanation only skims the surface of the subject. For a more thorough understanding, I refer you to "Please Understand Me," an essay on temperament styles by David Kiersey and Marilyn Bates, or "People Types and Tiger Stripes," by Gordon Lawrence. These books are available from most book stores.

The four pairs of personality preferences are:

> *Extroversion vs Introversion (E vs I)*
> *Intuition vs Sensation (N vs S)*
> *Thinking vs Feeling (T vs F)*
> *Judging vs Perceiving (J vs P)*

Let's now look in more detail at these personality pairs to get a better understanding of them.

Extroverted vs Introverted (E vs I)

Extroverted individuals tend to be sociable, action oriented, changing, sometimes impulsive, think best while talking, and like to work with people.

Introverted individuals tend to be territorial, reflect on matters, like to think things out before speaking, like to work alone or perhaps with only a few people, are reluctant to try something without understanding it completely, and like solitude.

Intuitive vs Sensory (N vs S)

Intuitive individuals like theory, are good at conceptualizing, like to use their imagination, enjoy finding new ways of doing things, are impatient with details, live life in anticipation, and are restless looking for something better in the future.

Sensing individuals are more interested in facts, like to solve problems in accepted ways, are good with details, and are more interested in experience than theory.

Thinking vs Feeling (T vs F)

Thinking individuals let logic rule their decisions, tend unknowingly to ignore the feelings of others, and are likely to make decisions based on facts alone.

Feeling individuals consider the feelings of people when making decisions, are concerned with other people's feelings in general, are upset by arguments, and quick to give recognition to others.

Judging vs Perception (J vs P)

Judging individuals like a planned predetermined way of life as opposed to a flexible spontaneous way, don't like to leave things up in the air but rather tend to look for closure on issues, like to finish one project before moving on to another, tend to decide things too quickly and are not easily swayed from an opinion.

Perceptive individuals like a flexible spontaneous way of life as opposed to a planned set way, become involved in many projects, may have difficulty finishing them, are indecisive and like to keep as may options open as possible.

It is interesting that a modern system of psychological typing can be based only on these four pairs. One might think that there should be more descriptive information for such a complicated exercise as determining one's personality type. However, this can be rationalized and possibly a little better understood by going through the following logic: Living our lives essentially involves making day-to-day decisions of all types, large and small: what clothes to wear, what to have for breakfast, what to do at work, whether to stop at the store on the way home, etc. In making a decision we may prefer to work alone if we are *introverted,* or to work with others if we are *extroverted.* We usually also have some kind of input. This input can be of a *intuitive* nature, that is, using our intuition, a dimension more abstract and beyond taking in the facts, or a *sensing* nature; that is, taking in facts by using our five senses. We then use that data to either make a *thinking* decision (using logic alone) or a *feeling* decision (considering the feelings of other people). The decision-making process itself can either be very *judging* (decisive) or *perceiving* (indecisive). Thus, it can be seen very simply, that these four pairs of preferences do adequately describe the manner in which we prefer to operate.

37

There has been a great deal of controversy as to exactly what Jung meant by the four pairs of preferences describing how people differ. It appears as though these controversies arose largely from his word choice, especially those of judging and perception. Judging does not imply a judging, critical person, but rather, to be decisive and inflexible. Perception, on the other hand, does not imply to perceive but rather indecisiveness, flexibility and spontaneity. Other definitions are: judging - preference for a fixed, orderly way of life; perception - preference for a spontaneous, flexible way of life, keeping as many options open as possible.

However, what is of importance is not the labels we assign to the preferences - what we call them - but what they actually represent. Since there are four pairs of preferences, there are sixteen (4x4) possible mathematical combinations of these. The sixteen combinations represent the psychological types. Every individual falls into one of these types. Each of the types has its own distinctive behavioral characteristics in terms of thinking and functioning.

An important point in discussing the preferences and the related personality types is that a person usually has a blend of both preferences for any pair, but favors one. For example, a person is almost never totally introverted or totally extroverted. Most individuals have elements of both introversion and extroversion but *usually* prefer to use one over the other. In some situations, however, depending upon the circumstances, individuals use their less-preferred process as well.

It is important to have a clear understanding of exactly what the preference pairs represent. The combination of the four preferences, one from each pair, that you tend to use in dealing with society or to conduct your life in general is essentially a "fingerprint" of your psychological type. Your psychological type classifies your style of operation.

Why does this seemingly simple combination of traits adequately describe or define something as complex as a personality type? The answer to this question is easily explained by using a little logic. The psychological types are described by eight related variables (the eight preferences), or four independent variables (the four preference pairs). Therefore, we have only to determine four (not eight) basic characteristics of a person to adequately characterize or classify his or her personality type. (For example, someone who is 80% extroverted must, by definition, be 20% introverted.) As we add variables, the amount of descriptive information that we gain is multiplied by some factor much larger that the increase in the number of variables. A synergistic effect takes place when a personality is described by many variables. The synergism results from the interactions between the variables themselves. Just as, in painting, an infinity of hues can be produced by mixing the primary colors, red, blue and yellow. The "mixing" of four character traits can also produce an infinite number of graduations of personalities.

Another way to look at this is that as we add variables we go from a very general to a very specific personality description. The following example will help to illustrate this point. Let's describe an individual. The first variable or preference pair that we might use in our description is extroverted versus introverted. Let's assume that the person is extroverted. This isn't very specific. Three-fourths of the people in the world are extroverted. Let's add the second variable, sensory/intuitive. Let's suppose he is sensory, i.e. he's practical and likes to deal with facts and details rather than theory. A good profession for this type of individual might be a banker: he likes to deal with people, likes to deal with facts and details, likes to deal with numbers. So, for the sake of argument, let's suppose he is a banker. As you can see, by adding that one additional variable, we went from a description accommodating three-fourths of the people of the world to a much more focused description - a banker-type. Now let's add a third variable, feeling/thinking. Let's suppose the individual is a feeling person. This might imply that he gets involved with the financial affairs of his customers far beyond the point that might be considered as pure business relationships. In other words, he may be the kind of person who would be likely to offer personal advice on financial and other matters in his client's life. Again, the description of the individual has become much more focused, containing much more specific information. Now let's add the final variable, perceptive/judging. Let's suppose he is a perceptive person, meaning that he likes a flexible, spontaneous way of life as opposed to a fixed routine or an orderly way of life. This might suggest that he prefers not to keep stringently regular hours at the bank, but would rather conduct his business by meeting his clients at other locations, say for lunch, dinner, or in the evening in a more sociable atmosphere.

As you can see, this example illustrates how a person's one variable description of extroverted, which is a description that fits three-fourths of the people of the world, may be accurately refined by the addition of only three more variables. Now the description becomes a person who is warm, feeling, involved in his clients' day-to-day lives, likes to deal with facts in a spontaneous way, and in general, does not like routine. This simple example illustrates the tremendous increase in descriptive information that is realized by adding a relatively few variables to a personality description used to generate the psychological types.

The sixteen psychological types, however, have been simplified. Individuals have elements of both preferences for each preference pair in their make-up. For example, if you are primarily extroverted, you also have some component of introversion in your personality. This is the case for the other three preference pairs as well. In other words, there would be a significant difference between two ENFP's (Extroverted - Intuitive - Feeling - Perceptive types) if one of them is extremely extroverted and intuitive and the other is marginally extroverted and intuitive. The latter individual would exhibit, in many situations, very strong signs of introversion and practicality. What this example demonstrates is that the sixteen psychological types represent a fairly coarse classification. A much more detailed typing scheme could be devised which would account for the degree of each preference. Such a scheme would contain a greater number of types and they would be more specific, containing more descriptive information. This refinement in typing would be very useful for some applications. However, it would be more complex, requiring more input and more detailed data interpretation. Such a typing system would probably be better applied using a computer to reduce and interpret the data.

The various combinations of preferences essentially program and control our interests, actions, and generally the way we like to operate in most situations. As a result, each of us falls into one of the sixteen categories which described his or her personality type. The Psychological Types Matrix shown at the end of this chapter gives a brief description of the characteristics of each of the sixteen psychological types.

This matrix was developed for this book and is intended to provide a shorthand notation of characteristics for each of the types. It is not intended to be comprehensive. One advantage of presenting the information and descriptions of the psychological types in the matrix format is that the similarities and differences between the various types are readily seen. For example, the first column (ESTJ, ESTP, ISTP, ISTJ) and the second column (ESFJ, ESFP, ISFP, ISFJ) represent types that are factual, practical, and detailed. The first column represents types that are analytical, logical, and impersonal, but the second column represents types that are sensitive, warm, and compassionate. From our preceding example of the banker you can imagine the large number of possibilities these various combinations of traits may lead to. The psychological types matrix is a condensed version of all the typing characteristics for all the types. You will find it extremely useful to describe a particular type or to compare types.

To determine your psychological type begin by going back to the answer sheet for the Entrepreneurial Aptitude Test that you took earlier (See Appendix A). Summarize the results

41

of the Answer Sheet by completing the Summary Sheet which follows the Answer Sheet. To do this, fill in the total number of A and B answers on the Answer Sheet (for sections I-VIII) by totaling the blocks in each row, across the page, and placing the "Totals" in the bold boxes on the right side of the page. Transfer these "Totals" to the following Summary Sheet in the equivalently labeled "Totals" boxes.

Your psychological type is indicated in Sections II, III, IV and V of the Summary Sheet of the Entrepreneurial Aptitude Test. In Section II, the "A" scores are for extroversion, and the "B" scores are for introversion. In Section III, the "A" scores are for thinking and the "B" scores are for feeling. In Section IV, the "A" scores are for judging and the "B" scores are for perceiving. In Section V, the "A" scores are for sensory and the "B" scores are for intuitive. Your type is thus determined by taking the higher score, either "A" or "B" for each pair and its related letter which is next to the *"Total"* boxes. (For example, in section II, if you have a larger number in box A than B, E for Extroverted will be the first letter of your psychological type) Your psychological type should now be memorized by you - we will refer to it much during the rest of this book.

To interpret your psychological type, use the psychological types matrix. It is interesting to see how your type compares to others that you associate with. Similarities or differences in types may explain differences or similarities in thinking, how individuals get along, the cause of disagreements and a multitude of other personal interactions that, on the surface, appear to have little or no rationale.

Even more significant is how your type compares with that of a successful entrepreneur. We also have distinctive attitudes and tend to think about things in our own particular manner. Because of this, we each have different aptitudes in the entrepreneurial arena. However, as we will show in the next chapter, there are ways to overcome our weaknesses, parlay our strengths, and enhance our entrepreneurial ability.

Psychological Types Matrix

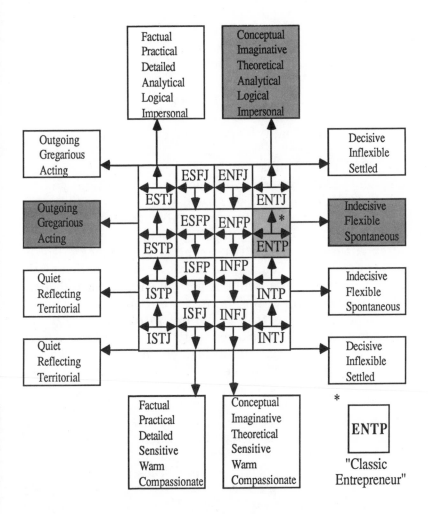

Look at the characteristics of your psychological type
Compare yourself to the "Classic Entrepreneur"

43

CHAPTER IV

Your Personality Type vs The Entrepreneur's

Becoming familiar with your psychological type can help you to understand better why you do some of the things you do, your likes and dislikes, your related strengths or weaknesses, particularly with respect to starting your own business. We have determined your psychological type from the Entrepreneurial Aptitude Test in the last chapter. Also, to establish a basis for comparison, we are going to define a role model in the form of a fictitious person, an individual that we will consider to be the perfect entrepreneur. On an entrepreneurial rating scale *(from one to one hundred),* this fictitious person will score a perfect hundred, the ideal business person, and we will call him or her the *classic entrepreneur.* Further, using some common sense, deductive reasoning and with little or no assumption, we will also determine the psychological type of the *classic entrepreneur.* By comparing your type with that of the *classic entrepreneur,* your personality traits that are likely to help you in the entrepreneurial arena will become apparent. Your personality traits that may hinder you are equally important and will also be discussed.

The issue of importance here is to be capable of making a meaningful and reliable psychological and operational comparison between the "classic entrepreneur" and the reader. This is the primary reason that the Entrepreneurial Aptitude Test was developed. The Entrepreneurial Aptitude test was developed based on research that established the key elements or ingredients of entrepreneurship. Other entrepreneurial tests and articles in the literature, to date, deal only with the symptoms of entrepreneurship - how do entrepreneurs operate? They do not address the issue of what are the necessary *inner* ingredients of entrepreneurship. These ingredients came from within the entrepreneur, his or her personality, and from his or her business operational styles. Subsequent research and testing was designed to test the accuracy of the test itself. In the final analysis, the profile of the "classic entrepreneur" is a complex aggregate of his or her personality traits, blended with business styles and attitudes coupled with more subtle symptoms resulting from the complex basic make-up of personality, background and attitudes.

The basic data to test your entrepreneurial ability and compare the reader to the *classic entrepreneur* comes from the Entrepreneurial Aptitude Test. All tests like the Entrepreneurial Aptitude Test are subject to a certain amount of error. We may answer in a manner that indicates the way we would like to be, rather than the way we are; or we may have difficulty in being completely objective about ourselves. Further, there may be errors induced by the statistical limitations of the test itself. For these reasons, this test and others like it, may not type you correctly. If you feel that your determined type is wrong in one or more of the preference areas, it probably is. You know yourself better than anyone else does. If a preference pair in your type is very evenly divided (approximately the same number for each preference), it is more susceptible to error. On the other hand, if the preference pair is very one-sided, the odds are that the typing is correct. The most accurate psychological typing test is probably the original Myers-Briggs test. If you have an opportunity to take that test, I urge you to do so. In spite of its limitations though, the Entrepreneurial Aptitude Test developed for this work, does type us accurately within an experimental error comparable to most tests like it. Further, the psychological typing portion of the test has been validated by comparing the results of statistically significant numbers of test subjects that were given both other accepted tests and the Entrepreneurial Aptitude Test. Further, if one or more of the preferences are incorrect, it is likely to be apparent to us as we read the description of the various types and we can compensate for that error.

What we will do now is use the psychological typing theory in reverse. The psychological typing theory is used to determine the personality traits of a subject, his or her psychological type, from the pattern of responses given in a typing exam. In this case, we know the characteristics of the subject, the *classic entrepreneur* and we would like to determine the entrepreneur's psychological type. In principle, we are simply using the typing theory in reverse. We know the characteristics of the entrepreneur and we are determining his type. We are not, as is usually done, using his psychological type to determine his characteristics.

Another way to explain this reasoning is that we are using the psychological typing techniques to type the *classic entrepreneur*. Once the *classic entrepreneur's* type is established we can discuss his or her personality traits, business attitudes and operational styles in exactly the same manner as we can for any one individual.

What is the psychological make-up of the *"classic entrepreneur"* ? How do we determine his or her psychological type? These are interesting questions. The answer to these questions describes a model entrepreneurial personality that we might choose to pattern our business lives after. When we describe the psychological type of the *"classic entrepreneur"*, this will provide a standard reference type to compare our own psychological type to, thus providing an indicator to measure our functional strengths and weaknesses in the entrepreneurial arena.

The following logic shows, that it is possible, with very little or no supposition, to determine the psychological type of the *"classic entrepreneur"*. To determine the classic entrepreneurial psychological type, we begin by returning to the four functional preference pairs that we discussed earlier:

Extroversion vs Introversion   *(E   vs   I)*

Intuition vs Sensation   *(N   vs   S)*

Thinking vs Feeling   *(T   vs   F)*

Judging vs Perceiving   *(J   vs P)*

The next logical step is to examine each preference pair, comparing the preference choices to typical entrepreneurial behavior.

E vs I - Extroversion *(outgoing and gregarious)* is definitely a trait more associated with entrepreneurship than is *introversion (quiet and reflecting)*. In fact, there are other characteristics of the entrepreneur, closely related to extroversion, some of these are: social charm, charisma and the ability to win people over. The entrepreneur is a leader, a team builder and uses every resource that he possibly can, including people. Extroversion is a trait that is a great asset to the entrepreneur.

N vs S - In this preference pair, *intuition (conceptual, imaginative and theoretical)* is also a preference more associated with entrepreneurship than is *sensation (factual, practical and detailed)*. In fact the typical entrepreneur is very intuitive, often strongly relying on a gut feeling or an unusually accurate hunch. The entrepreneur also uses his intuition to reduce the element of risk, at least in his or her own mind. Risk is introduced by not having enough facts to know an outcome of a particular situation. Intuition can play an important role in such a situation by substituting intuition for fact - if only to provide courage. Intuition is also associated with the ability to develop strategy, since subtle options may be apparent to entrepreneurs.

***T vs F - Thinking** (analytical, logical and impersonal)* is definitely a trait more associated with entrepreneurship than is *feeling (sensitive, warm and compassionate)*. The typical entrepreneur has a good sense for formulating strategy which is closely related to sound logic. The entrepreneur has an analytical, logical mind which weighs all of the options and proceeds with the one most likely to succeed.

***J vs P* -** When considering this pair, *perceiving (indecisive, spontaneous and flexible)* is also a preference more associated with entrepreneurship than is *judging (decisive, settled and inflexible)*. P's are probably better "risk takers" than J's. Studies have also shown that one of the most noticeable differences between entrepreneurs and executives is that entrepreneurs tend to leave options open and remain flexible, while executives tend to make issue-closing decisions. Once these decisions are made, executives tend to stick to them, entrepreneurs don't. The entrepreneur is ready to change direction whenever necessary, heading off in a new direction that may make sense to him at the moment, to satisfy his newly formulated plan. This style of operation has been referred to as *goal-less* planning -- it may be related to an ability to deal with risk spontaneously. In contrast to the other preference pairs however, a blend of perception and judgment is probably more necessary for entrepreneurship than for the other preference pairs. In many entrepreneurial ventures, *decisiveness* is often a valuable trait.

What we have unambiguously shown is that of the sixteen possible psychological types, ***Extroversion, Intuitive, Thinking, Perceiving (ENTP) represents the personal "fingerprint" of the "classic entrepreneur"***. We can reliably narrow our choice to this single type. How does your psychological type compare with the ***ENTP*** type? A close match indicates that you have psychological traits that will be assets in the entrepreneurial arena. Differences do not mean that you cannot be a successful entrepreneur. Rather, they identify areas in which you will not function easily. Keep in mind also, that approximately only _five in one hundred people have the ideal ENTP entrepreneurial personality_ - if you don't, you're not alone. There are many successful entrepreneurs who aren't ENTPs - you can be too.

It should be emphasized that the ESTP type also has may qualities of the _classic entrepreneur_. However, this type is usually better at promoting existing ventures rather than starting new ones. Their pragmatic nature limits the innovative vision necessary to orchestrate the spawning of new ventures. Further, we are not concluding that introverted, sensation, feeling and judging personalities cannot be successful entrepreneurs. Rather, what we are indicating is that these traits are not typically strengths of the _classic entrepreneur_. Individuals having these traits should be aware of this.

Changing your personality, your psychological traits, is similar to changing your PSE, both have taken a lifetime to develop and both can be influenced but are difficult to change, if not impossible. Your psychological traits can be influenced though - in a manner similar to instituting change in your PSE. Your personality can be influenced by _external forces_. One external force that can complement all of your psychological traits is to team with an individual who has the traits, the skills, that you lack. This is a typical move of the entrepreneur. Entrepreneurs are capable of providing the needed spark to a group of individuals working as a team in a venture. They do not necessarily have all of the needed skills themselves. Surround yourself with people who have the skills you need.

Interfacing with people leads to relationships - all types of relationships. Personal success includes enjoying valued personal relationships. Business success usually also includes interacting with people and the development of many relationships. As we have mentioned these are often established out of necessity and a good example is the teaming of individuals with complementary entrepreneurial skills to start a business. Our personality types also play an important role in these relationships.

No man (or woman) is an island - we are all involved in many relationships throughout our lives. The compatibility and the combined effectiveness of two individuals when teaming in a business arrangement involves many factors: similar likes and dislikes, their strengths and weaknesses, their styles of operation and their varied experiences. These elements are also some of the information bits that make up your sphere. The contents of your sphere then, also influence the quality of your relationships.

When two people have a close personal relationship, their two spheres gradually, over time, merge into one. For example, if they get married, their independent spheres slowly combine and eventually become one. Ultimately, they have the same friends, live in the same home, drive the same automobiles, have similar schedules, etc. Further, their composite sphere is usually larger than either of the initial spheres. However, they probably will retain remnants of their original spheres since they may have separate careers and friends.

In business teaming relationships, there is also an overlapping of spheres, but usually only in specific areas pertaining to business. This *composite sphere* may also be enriched in the entrepreneurial or business areas resulting from the pooling of complementary entrepreneurial skills and resources. Since this is true, one way to measure mutual enrichment of both parties, in a teaming arrangement, is to compare the resources of the initial isolated spheres with those of the new composite sphere. Individuals teaming with unlike spheres will probably be more complementary. Therefore, entering into a business relationship with someone unlike yourself, can be an interesting, as well as a rewarding experience.

There's a saying that opposites attract - they do. Psychologists agree that we tend to gravitate to individuals who are unlike ourselves. Why this occurs is not clearly understood. However, it's as though we can find that *other side of ourselves* through that *opposite* person; the side that we never had. For example, an introverted person may well associate with an outgoing, flamboyant type. He or she senses that association with that person will provide some missing element in his or her life. Fortunately, this tendency of opposites attracting, provides a natural catalyst to promote both enriching personal and business relationships by facilitating the combining of complementary skills.

There is however a potential pitfall in these relationships. Opposite personalities may encounter compatibility problems. If this happens, our instincts may encourage us to attempt to modify the other persons behavior - to make the person more like ourselves. In other words, that which attracted us to the other person at the outset, we now would like to change. If this happens, we must resist this urge. We must also realize that the blend of unlike qualities that may be causing the incompatibility, is exactly what may make a personal relationship or new business flourish. Even though opposites attract, it is usually *easier* to enter into a personal or business relationship with someone much like yourself. Initially, you simply feel more comfortable with a person who thinks and operates the way you do. Remember, however, these relationships are not nearly as potentially rewarding.

There are other outside forces besides teaming that can help you to influence your psychological traits. If you are not a logical (thinking) or conceptual (intuitive) person another external force that may help you is the use of advisors, preferably experts from outside your PSE. Make it a habit to discuss new areas of endeavor and strategy with others that can help you. Introversion and judgmental (inflexibility) are more difficult to influence by external forces. Being aware of your behavior in your every-day activities, however, may trigger responses that may foster more extroversion and improve your flexibility. Even a little change in these traits will go a long way toward improving your effectiveness in the business area.

Interpersonal Skills - The relationship and teaming

discussions lead us naturally into an important and intriguing area - that of interpersonal skills. One of the very distinctive traits of many entrepreneurs is their ability to *win people over - they have a way with people.* In other words, either naturally or by working at it, they have developed good interpersonal skills.

Interpersonal skills may be defined as those skills that we use in our relationships with others that help us to work productively and effectively with them, while enhancing our rapport with them. As Dale Carnegie points out in his book "How to Win Friends and Influence People," this should not be confused with manipulating others - a sense of sincerity toward the other individual is the distinguishing factor.

Interpersonal skills are important in all walks of life and careers; this is especially true in the business and entrepreneurial arenas. Mark Stevens in his book "Small Business Mistakes and How to Avoid Them" states: *"Turn off even your best patrons with rude or inferior service and you've lost a friend to the competition. Don't be fooled into thinking that today's crowd will necessarily be there tomorrow. Just give them a reason to turn away and the competition will do the rest"* . There is no doubt about it, good interpersonal skills can often mean the difference between success and failure in business. There are few of us that do not require interaction at the personal level in our jobs, our careers, or simply to exist comfortably in our personal lives. Whether we are attempting to develop an effective customer service program, or perhaps just a good rapport with our fellow workers, our customers or our friends - good interpersonal skills will help us throughout our lives.

One good way to begin developing interpersonal skills is to understand others. A prerequisite to understanding others is the understanding of ourselves - the development of a sense of self-awareness. Feedback from others is a good way to develop your personal self-awareness. We must always keep in mind that how we are perceived by others may not be in agreement with how we perceive ourselves. Remember also, as shocking as

52

it may seem, how others perceive us is reality - our perception has little to do with it. Knowing and understanding our own strengths and weaknesses, our own feelings, will help us to understand others and will subsequently help us to deal with others.

Robert Conklin in his book "How To Get People To Do Things", expressed the three "A's" of interpersonal skills: Acceptance, Approval and Appreciation. These can be accomplished by: making others feel important, looking for the good qualities of people, making others feel wanted, make others feel capable, make others feel good about themselves, and by being positive, polite and patient. Although it almost sounds like good common sense, it is surprising the problems, misunderstandings, conflict, and loss of productivity that originate because these simple philosophies are not understood. Your interpersonal skills, in a complex manner, may also be related to your psychological type. As we mentioned before, they are also related to how you view yourself.

Is your personal description, or the way you view yourself, compatible with the Entrepreneurial Aptitude Test typing? Don't forget that for each of the preference pairs, you have elements of both traits in your personality. Under some conditions or some situations in you life, you will revert to your less preferred traits. Remember also that what makes a person an entrepreneur is not his or her psychological type but rather the **blend** of traits included in his or her type and other traits as well. The preferences introversion, feeling, sensory and judgmental also play a role in every entrepreneur and most likely contribute to his or her effectiveness.

It would also be good to review the sixteen psychological types matrix presented earlier, again mentally emphasizing the classic entrepreneur (ENTP) type. Also, pay attention to your own psychological type, considering how you are similar to and how you differ from other psychological types. Remember, to achieve success you must interact with people, and the differences in psychological types indicate that people may think and act differently.

It is interesting to observe how well these "classic entrepreneurial" typing results agree with the model of the personal sphere of equilibrium. The psychological typing results that we derived here basically indicate that introversion, sensation, feeling and judging are preferences that would not typically be found in the classical entrepreneurial psychological type. In the PSE model, introversion and judging (inflexibility) indicate poor outer personal sphere adaptability, necessary traits to perform many life-changing activities. The feeling and sensation preferences would indicate that an individual would prefer to function with feeling in his sphere, probably with friends and acquaintances, emphasizing details. On the other hand, logic and intuition are traits that may be lacking and are necessary in planning overall strategy to operate out of his or her sphere. The important point is that the psychological typing results and the personal sphere of equilibrium results are totally compatible and, in fact, reinforce each other.

CHAPTER V

Your Operational Style

To this point in the book, we have identified several traits which are likely to affect your ability to achieve any goal, to find success, or to enter the business arena. In fact, if in general you have difficulty in accomplishing things and perhaps don't consider yourself successful, this is almost certainly linked to your inability and possibly even your extreme reluctance to work outside of your sphere. This chapter especially focuses on individuals who tend to have this difficulty. Such individuals, almost without exception, will make statements like: "I know I should do better, but I really can't seem to", or, "I always wanted to be in business for myself, but I just don't seem to have the initiative to make it happen."

There is a striking difference between people who are successful and people who aren't. People who are successful have a noticeably easier time operating through their sphere/outer-world interface. They may not like it, but they are quite capable of it. In some cases, they may even be at ease in dealing with the world outside of their sphere. In sharp contrast, people who can't deal effectively through that interface have a hard time accomplishing anything. Rather, they feel very comfortable in and rarely leave their sphere. To paraphrase this, they associate with their life routine, a strong sense of security.

The ease with which we can move out of our sphere has

to do with several things. An important one is our background - the exposure that we experienced as we grew up. If we had broad exposure, it will naturally be much easier to make excursions from our sphere. This is true because we are familiar with many more areas outside of our sphere and we know what to expect *out there;* we are more confident. On the other hand, if our exposure was limited, stepping out of the sphere is more difficult. Moving out of our spheres is also related to our personality traits, our psychological types that we discussed earlier. For example, an extrovert has an advantage over an introvert in this area. In fact, the *classic entrepreneurial* personality type ENTP, in general, has traits that facilitate his or her moving from the sphere of equilibrium with greater ease.

What's the secret to getting things done? There are several necessary elements that are included in every accomplishment process. To get a better idea of what these are, it might be beneficial to explore how one accomplishes anything - how you do anything. Although you don't usually think of it so systematically, there are four basic steps that you go through either consciously or subconsciously when you do anything. If you have a better understanding of what these steps are and then, if you can't seem to accomplish something, the step which represents the bottleneck (or snag) may be easier to identify. These steps are:

Step 1.   **Concept** (the idea)
Step 2.   **Strategy** (general thinking of related logic and options)
Step 3.   **Plan** (detailed planning of how to do it)
Step 4.   **Implementation** (the actual doing of it - discipline is a strong consideration here)

You go through these steps, usually subconsciously, but you go through them just the same, for any accomplishment. This can be shown by the following example of starting a business:

Idea --------------- "I'd like to start my own business - a restaurant - to work for myself".

Strategy ---------- "Health foods are popular - there's a market for that type of restaurant - I know about health foods and restaurants - I'll open one".

Plan --------------- "I'll find a location - negotiate a lease - think of a name - borrow some capital and open one".

Implementation -- Actually opening the restaurant.

This example is demonstrating that these steps are necessary in doing anything, even starting a business. This is especially true in satisfying more complicated activities such as the accomplishment of lifelong goals.

Accomplishing goals outside your sphere also requires these same four steps, except that, as we said before, it's more difficult for you to execute them. Since you are most likely better at some steps than others, your weaknesses may act as stumbling blocks in accomplishing specific ones. When applying this reasoning to starting your business, remember that your main concern is the execution of business-origination steps outside your PSE. The mechanics of these steps are essential in **any** accomplishment process, and your ability to perform them is related to your psychological type.

Because of this, an "Operational Style Matrix" was developed for this book. Your operational style is shown in sections V, VI, VII and VIII of the Entrepreneurial Aptitude Test Summary Sheet. How does your operational style compare to that of the "Classic Entrepreneur" shown on the following Operational Style Matrix?

Operational Style Matrix

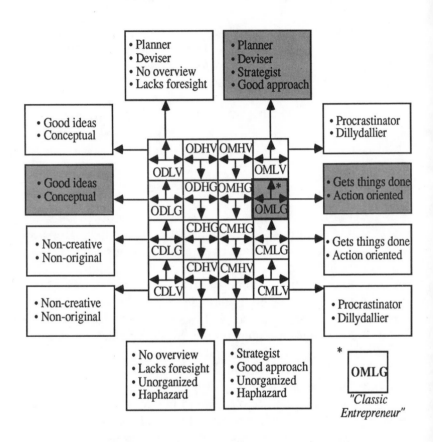

The four operational steps needed to accomplish any goal or venture are discussed in more detail:

Step 1 - Idea or Concept

If you are to do anything, you have to have an idea. In other words, the thought must pass through your mind that you are going to do whatever it is that you wish to accomplish. This initial step, the concept or idea, is often taken for granted. It's taken for granted because it usually happens automatically - an idea usually just "pops" into your head. But this step is of utmost importance. The seed of the idea had to come from somewhere. *Example:* If you were never exposed to entrepreneurial activities and the potential benefits and self-satisfaction that can be derived from them, you probably wouldn't be interested in starting your own business.

Step 2 - Strategy

The second step in getting something accomplished is strategy. In this step you decide why and how you are going to proceed. *For example,* in the health food restaurant case, your strategic thinking might go something like this: "I've always wanted to go into business for myself and I really like working with the public. There is a market in that area. I can earn a good income by running such a business and I'd enjoy it." This kind of strategic thinking is usually very simple, very fundamental, and to the point. It is usually at this stage that you weigh the advantages and disadvantages and review the options available. In most cases, it is in this step that you decide if you will carry through your idea or not.

Step 3 - Plan

In the plan you outline the details of exactly how you will accomplish whatever it is you set out to do. In the case of the opening of a health food restaurant, it may include such things as: deciding where the start-up money will come from, how much is needed, at what interest rate, what salaries will be drawn from the business, what the rent will be, what are the estimated utilities, exactly where it will be located, what you will do in the way of advertising, how many employees you will have, etc. You might think of the plan as a road map containing a detailed route and step-by-step instructions for meeting your objective.

Step 4 - Implementation

Implementation is the actual doing of the tasks that are involved in accomplishing your objective. The implementation step appears to be relatively straightforward. You simply do whatever you outlined in the operational plan. If you follow through and complete all the steps outlined in the plan, you will accomplish your objective.

There are however, two areas that especially affect how well you implement any plan. These are: how you manage your time, and self-discipline. These are somewhat interrelated and often are the root-cause of failure during implementation. Our father used the expression "If you want to get something done, ask a busy person to do it." There is a lot of truth to this. Busy people tend to be better organized and therefore manage somehow to find time to get things done, no matter how much they have to do. Usually, the reason for this is that they are disciplined and they manage their time better.

This leads to another consideration when describing people who seem to have that special ability to "get things done." Often they appear to be impulsive - but are they? There are two types of impulsive people. The first is the truly impulsive individual characterized as acting before he really thinks things out. This is not the type of individual that we are referring to. It is the other type, who might be better described as *determined* to get things done and therefore, appears to be impulsive. Is this determination a good trait; or does it cause confusion? The answer to this is that at times it may cause confusion. On the other hand, in doing most things, you usually have a great deal of time and energy invested in laying the groundwork, both physically and psychologically. If you don't implement at the proper time, this effort, that laying of the groundwork, may be lost. It is for this reason that the impulsive types want to finish something, at all cost, once they begin. They realize that after a certain point is reached, a little more effort in the way of implementation will finish the project.

Another way to consider this reasoning is that it may be fine and even sensible to let something go for a day, a week, or even a month and then finish it. But the question is - are you certain that you will get back to it or are you running the risk of never getting it done? When you walk away from a project, you are really taking a chance that you'll never finish it. Perhaps the discipline that the *"get-things-done"* people exhibit is somewhat the result of their being aware of this. Another way to classify this category of people is to describe them as spontaneous. Success-oriented individuals and entrepreneurs tend to be capable of quickly getting excited about a new potential endeavor.

Many books have been written on time management. Time is a resource that cannot be replaced. Once it is used, it is gone forever. To use your time effectively is to use your time doing the important things in your life. Time management experts have suggested a number of ways to help you do this. There are two especially important points. The first is to itemize the things you want to get done in the order of their importance and then spend your time on the most important ones first. In this manner, when you run out of time - and we always seem to - you'll have the most important things already finished. The second is, if there are a relatively large number of small tasks and several larger ones of about equal importance, do the small ones first to simplify your schedule. In other words, reduce the number of things with which you must be concerned - in other words, make your life a little easier.

To manage your time effectively, to do the most important things first, requires self-discipline. The most important things aren't necessarily the things you like to do. What is self-discipline? What is its role in this life-changing or new entrepreneurial direction reasoning? To understand discipline and the power it has over our lives, let's recall the concept of equilibrium that we discussed earlier. Discipline represents another example of an equilibrium that you are living with. With everything you do, in every day of your life, _you are involved in maintaining a delicate balance between self-discipline and self-gratification_ (self-indulgence). At times the equilibrium is shifted in the discipline direction and you are more productive. At other times the equilibrium is shifted toward the self-gratification direction and you ignore that little voice within your head telling you to do what you promised yourself you would do.

We all maintain that delicate balance, that equilibrium between self-discipline and self-gratification. But, what controls the intensity of our discipline? Why are some individuals so disciplined that they seem to be able to accomplish a great deal, while others usually have their equilibrium shifted toward the self-gratification side? Such individuals have difficulty accomplishing anything, regardless of their abilities. The answer lies in their value systems. It's that simple. **Your level of discipline is controlled by your value system.** Your values set your priorities and your priorities control your drive, or discipline, to do or to accomplish anything.

Very often if you have difficulty getting something done no matter how well you plan and how good your intentions, the problem may not lie in your ability to execute, but rather in your motivation or drive. In spite of what you may think you want, you really don't value it enough. You don't have the discipline to accomplish it, because deep within you, it does not rank very high on your priority list. You simply don't value it enough. In that case, your discipline/self-gratification equilibrium is shifted toward the self-gratification side. Subconsciously, you can't be bothered with doing it. A good example of this is that many people who couldn't quit smoking do so immediately after they have a heart attack.

The question that this reasoning is suggesting is: how badly do you really want to start your own business? Is it something that you really value? Only you can answer that question.

Discipline is a necessary prerequisite to accomplish anything. You not only have to make up your mind to accomplish something, but you really have to value the results. If you can't seem to accomplish a goal no matter how good your intentions and how well equipped you are to perform the task, the root-cause of your problem may be your value system. If that's the case, you'd better change your course or reevaluate your objective. Value systems are difficult to change, they took years to develop and will take years to change, if ever. *Value systems evolve through life and they are usually not quickly changed.*

Your personality traits, the four preferences of your psychological type, also affect your achievement potential in the four accomplishment steps. The Entrepreneurial Aptitude Test was also designed to measure your achievement potential in each of the these steps. Your potential in these steps, (your ability to get things done) and how this relates to your personality traits will be discussed in the next chapter.

CHAPTER VI

Self-analysis

The Entrepreneurial Aptitude Test (or E Q Test) which you took earlier was designed to measure your natural inclination toward business by: 1) estimating your ability to make excursions from your sphere (outer PSE adaptability), 2) comparing your psychological type with that of the *classic entrepreneur* (ENTP), and 3) determining your attitude and potential in each of the four operational steps (idea, strategy, plan, and implementation - discipline is included in this area as well). These three areas contribute to your entrepreneurial aptitude. These areas also provide the basis for the factors included in the entrepreneurial success equation which numerically measures your business aptitude, on a scale from zero to a hundred. This equation will be presented later.

Your preferred processes are responsible for your developing specialized skills and interests which produce characteristic habits, attitudes, and traits. Because of these specializations, you're better at doing some things than others. The Entrepreneurial Aptitude Test can be used not only to determine your potential in each of the operational steps, but also to determine how comfortable you are with them because of your personality traits and background. Your results may be a strong indication of the operational steps that you perform well in and also those needing special attention and effort (missing pieces in your sphere). We will interpret your outer PSE

64

"Self Evaluation is accomplished by measuring your natural inclination toward business by: 1) estimating your ability to make excursions from your sphere (outer PSE adaptability), 2) comparing your psychological type with that of the classic entrepreneur (ENTP), and 3) determining your attitude and potential in each of the four operational steps."

adaptability and achievement results in this chapter. Your personality preferences will be discussed to the extent that they affect outer PSE adaptability and the operational steps. The results of the E Q Test are intended to provide enlightenment and guidance in accomplishing your entrepreneurial life changing activities.

Let's now take a more detailed look at what we can expect to find in your Entrepreneurial Aptitude Test Summary Sheet. The areas of interest that we will look at in detail are: the outer PSE adaptability area:

- **outer PSE adaptability**

the personality traits areas:

- **extroverted/introverted**
- **thinking/feeling**
- **judging/perceiving**
- **sensory/intuitive**

and the operational traits areas:

- **idea attitude**
- **strategy attitude**
- **planning attitude**
- **implementation attitude**

Begin by going back to the Summary Sheet for the Entrepreneurial Aptitude Test that you took earlier (see Appendix A). The personality traits section, (II-V) was discussed previously. As we discuss each of these areas, be honest with yourself regarding your strengths and weaknesses. You know yourself better than anyone else does. The important consideration is to attempt to understand yourself in terms of how well you operate in each of the areas. The A or B box in each column of the Entrepreneurial Aptitude Test Summary Sheet with the larger number represents either a strength, weakness, or personality preference. The personality traits (sections II through V) indicate your similarities or differences to the *classic entrepreneurial* personality type. Your personality type also influences sections I and V through VIII but in a more indirect manner.

Outer PSE Adaptability (I - Entrepreneurial Aptitude Test)

Outer PSE Adaptability is an important factor in affecting life-changing activities (like starting your business). If the indicator shows this to be one of your strengths, you probably have an attitude that will help you to work in new unfamiliar areas. On the other hand, if the indicator shows this as a weakness, be aware that it may be more difficult for you to initiate life-changing activities. Remember though, nobody is entirely comfortable while operating outside of his or her sphere. By definition, our sphere is our comfort zone, and we all have a comfort zone, although this zone may be larger for some of us than for others. Also remember that this is an *entrepreneurial skill* that you can learn.

There are three personality preferences that naturally may be associated with helping you to operate outside your sphere. These are **extroversion, intuition**, and **perception**. Incidentally, all of these preferences are included in the *classic entrepreneur* ENTP type. Other preferences may also contribute, but these three are most strongly related to working outside of your sphere. Extroversion is included, since working in new areas means working with new people, a strength of an extrovert. An intuitive person may also have an edge in working out of his or her sphere since an imaginative personality is one that facilitates accepting and adapting to new ideas.

A perceptive person, by definition, is a person who is spontaneous and flexible, two traits that are compatible with being willing to work in and adapt to unfamiliar environments. If working out of your sphere is a strength, you may well have the personality traits described. If working out of your sphere is a strength and you aren't extroverted, intuitive and perceptive, this is probably an indication that you have an extremely well-rounded background with much depth. On the other hand, if you are extroverted, intuitive and perceptive but working out of your sphere is a weakness, it should be relatively easy for you to build strength in this area - you have the natural resources. In most cases, individuals will have some but not all of the personality traits associated with moving out of their spheres. The important point is to be aware or your strengths and weaknesses as they apply to moving into new areas in your life and to use your strengths to their fullest and try to work around your weaknesses. Being aware of your weaknesses is a good first step to dealing with them. Knowing the missing pieces in the puzzle of your sphere will also be a great advantage. Let's now take a look at some of the other areas emphasized in the Entrepreneurial Aptitude Test.

<u>Personality Traits</u> (II through V - Entrepreneurial Aptitude Test)

These play an important role directly and by influencing the other sections. The important comparison is how well your psychological type compares with that of the *classic entrepreneur* (ENTP).

<u>Operational Traits</u>
Idea Attitude (V - Entrepreneurial Aptitude Test)

Having the idea is the first step to accomplishing anything. It is the seed of any accomplishment. Notice that the idea attitude and the intuitive/sensory personality preference are

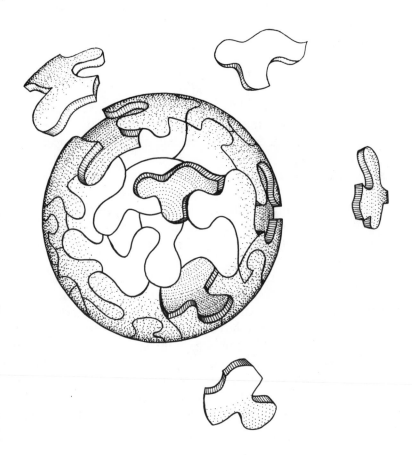

*"Being aware of your weaknesses is a good first step to dealing with them. Knowing the **missing pieces in the puzzle of your sphere** will also be a great advantage."*

69

superimposed on the Entrepreneurial Aptitude Test Answer Summary Sheet. Intuitiveness and an idea attitude usually go together. Notice also that intuitiveness is a preference of the *classic entrepreneurial type,* ENTP. If the E Q Test shows that your idea attitude is a strength, you are an idea person, visualizing yourself in new situations, in new roles. If your idea attitude is a weakness, you are probably a sensory, more down-to-earth person. It should be emphasized however, that traits of both the "idea person" and the "detailed person" can be useful in entrepreneurship. The idea person, however, probably better represents an entrepreneur. Remember, even if your idea attitude is a strength, that conceptualizing in areas out of the domain of your sphere is somewhat more difficult. If the E Q Test shows that your idea attitude is a weakness, reaching out for help in starting and running your business is even more necessary. Remember, life-changing concepts or ideas will more likely than not come from outside your sphere, i.e., outside your established circle of friends and acquaintances. Don't limit the source of your good ideas.

The single personality trait that is most associated with conceptualizing or ideas is **intuitiveness**. Intuitive personalities are imaginative, theoretical, and in general, "look to the future". If you have an intuitive personality, the conceptual process will come to you naturally. Remember however, that it is difficult to conceptualize in areas you know little about. Although important, in most cases, the conceptual step is not a serious problem in accomplishing goals. It is usually more of a problem in the strategy and planning stages - the setting of goals.

Strategy Attitude (VI - Entrepreneurial Aptitude Test)

If the Entrepreneurial Aptitude Test indicates that your strategy attitude is a strength, you will most likely feel at ease in formulating a basic strategic plan to accomplish your goals. That is, you will have a knack for examining the options available and arriving at a logical approach to reach your objectives. If the Entrepreneurial Aptitude Test shows that your strategy attitude is a weakness, you will most likely have difficulty determining a suitable strategy. Details are not important at this stage; the overall strategy that will be employed is your primary focus. One thing you should remember is that in any endeavor there are usually a number of different ways to proceed. Again, as was the case in the concept stage, it will probably be a good idea to get help in formulating your strategy from sources outside of your sphere - those who are more familiar with various aspects of your new venture. When at all possible, get advice and help from experts working in the field of interest.

The two personality traits linked with the ability to formulate strategy are **intuitiveness** and **thinking,** these preferences are also included in the *classic entrepreneurial* type ENTP. Strategic planning is simply a logical approach to selecting the best of a number of theoretical possibilities to accomplish your objectives. If you are intuitive and thinking, that is, a logical thinking person, you will certainly have an advantage in this area. The strategy you formulate could well mean the difference between success and failure.

The strategy step takes an idea and provides the ingredient (the manner in which to proceed) necessary to make it a reality. Sound strategy is of paramount importance and it is also the step at which many new efforts fail. The reason for this is that many times it is difficult to formulate strategy about something we know little about. Coming up with an idea is one thing. That may be possible even if it's in an unfamiliar area. But following through with that idea, formulating strategy (deciding how to proceed), becomes exceedingly more difficult. This brings us back to the logic that there are many ideas but relatively few of them actually become a reality. This is because, strategies needed to take concepts and develop them into tangible entities are usually much rarer than the ideas that initiated those concepts.

Planning Attitude   (VIII - Aptitude Test)

As we said before, your plan contains the details of how to accomplish the strategy outlined to meet your objective, perhaps starting your business. The operating plan represents the breaking down of the total project into detailed steps and describing the manner in which each of these steps will be accomplished. If the E Q Test shows that your planning attitude is a strength, you will be at ease in establishing an overall operating plan to accomplish your objective. On the other hand, if the E Q Test shows that this is a weakness, then you may have some problem with the detailed plan. The detailed plan is important because it provides the guidance for your day-to-day activities. The detailed plan is also sometimes called a "plan of action". It may be long or short, may be written, or it may simply be a mental exercise. This depends on how you like to operate. There is a great advantage however, to a written plan - it tends to be more detailed and it can be referred to daily. A written plan also exhibits a greater sense of self commitment. The important thing though, is not the way the plan is written or verbalized or even mentally reviewed, but rather the completeness of the plan and its ability to suitably outline what you want to accomplish.

The personality traits that naturally go along with detailed planning are **sensory, thinking** and **judgmental**. It should be emphasized that the sensory and judgmental traits are not preferences of the *"classic entrepreneur"*. This may help indicate why *entrepreneurs are often better at starting companies than running them.* Detail planning and implementation are not necessarily strong points of the entrepreneur. If you have these planning traits, you will probably feel at ease with the detailed planning exercise A sensory person likes to deal with the facts, and facts are usually associated with details. A thinking person is logical, and it's always advantageous to have a logical sequence of events in any plan. A judgmental person is one who likes a planned and orderly way of life, and therefore, by his very nature is adept at detailed planning. If you are an intuitive person, the odds are you won't be very patient with the detailed planning exercise. Remember though, you have to go through the detailed planning exercise only once in your venture. The detailed planning step is important; it is the recipe or plan of action that you will follow throughout your business start-up period.

Implementation Attitude (VIII - Entrepreneurial Aptitude Test)

You are finally at the implementation stage, the actual starting of your business. One thing you want to remember about implementation is that many enterprises begin with good intentions and are somehow bogged down because we don't follow through. We don't follow through for a number of reasons, one of which - and probably the main one - is a lack of self-discipline. Remember the equilibrium we talked about before, between self-discipline and self-gratification? We are constantly faced with this equilibrium almost every day of our lives. Remember too that the equilibrium is shifted toward the discipline side if we highly value our goal - starting our business. In other words, we have to want to own our own business badly enough. If you are having difficulty in starting your business, do not overlook the possibility that the cause of the problem might be your value system. This may be the time for some *"soul-searching"* to sort this out in your mind.

The other area where you may run into problems with implementation is in managing your time. If you are attempting to accomplish a life-changing objective, like starting a business, it can only be achieved by spending considerable time working out of your sphere. Self-discipline is intertwined with managing your time, since in many cases you may rather spend your time in other activities.

If the E Q Test shows that your implementation attitude is a strength, then you are the type of person who can usually follow through with projects. On the other hand, if the E Q Test shows this area as a weakness, perhaps getting things done is more difficult for you. It is important that you determine why it is a weakness. Is it because you lack discipline, or is it because you don't manage your time well, or is it for some other reason? If you can come to grips with this and identify the source, then you have a much better chance of following through with your new venture. Understanding the problem is the first step in solving it.

The personality traits that can be associated with implementation in new endeavors are **extroversion** and **judgmental**. Judgmental is not a typical preference of the entrepreneur, again indicating that entrepreneurs are often typically better at starting new ventures than at running them. On the other hand, a judgmental person may want to consider purchasing and running an existing business. In carrying out a venture, extroversion is a definite advantage in implementation outside your sphere. Similarly, a judgmental attitude (fixed, orderly routine) is compatible with step-by-step execution of the detailed plan that was formulated in the planning stage. It may also be argued that perception, the trait describing the spontaneous, flexible style of the entrepreneur may be equally as effective for implementing some ventures - especially high risk ventures.

Discipline and time management intermixed with the personality traits described play a complex role in the implementation step. Poor implementation is the cause of many failures of new businesses. If you have a problem with implementation, attempt to identify its source and focus on correcting it. Be especially concerned with self discipline and time management.

To start or run a business is going to require your executing the idea, strategy, planning and implementation steps for your new enterprise outside of your sphere. The key is to know your strengths and weaknesses as indicated in the Entrepreneurial Aptitude Test and to try to build on the strengths and as much as possible correct your weaknesses. Use the E Q Test for guidance, not only to establish your operational traits but to highlight your personality traits as well. Starting a successful business is a matter of using entrepreneurial skills in areas where you probably don't like to work - outside your personal sphere of equilibrium.

CHAPTER VII

The Entrepreneurial Success Equation

We have identified three basic ingredients contributing to success in the entrepreneurial arena. An important one is your ability to work outside your personal sphere of equilibrium; we have labeled this trait your **"Outer PSE Adaptability"**. Working outside your PSE is important, since no matter how good your intentions, no matter how talented you are, life-changing events, especially in the business world, usually initiate beyond your sphere/world interface. The other two ingredients of success have to do with how well you function in and out of your sphere. Your **"Personality Traits"** (your psychological type) play an important role and the final ingredient has to do with how you get things done by execution of the four operational steps: idea, strategy, planning and implementation. How well you execute these steps is a result of your **"Operational Traits."** Discipline also affects your ability to perform these steps, especially implementation. The three ingredients of entrepreneurial success may be summarized as:

- **Outer PSE Adaptability**
- **Entrepreneurial Personality Traits**
- **Operational Traits (includes discipline)**

It should be emphasized that the following equation measures your ability to *change* your life in such a manner as to enable you to achieve success in the entrepreneurial arena. It does not necessarily measure how successful you are now. Your propensity or tendency for success in business (through change) may be expressed by the following equation:

ENTREPRENEURIAL SUCCESS =

(1) OUTER PSE ADAPTABILITY +

(2) ENTREPRENEURIAL PERSONALITY TRAITS +

(3) BUSINESS OPERATIONAL TRAITS

*"We have identified **three basic ingredients** contributing to success in the entrepreneurial arena."*

77

To gain insight into your entrepreneurial success formula, a numerical version of this equation has been developed. To determine your entrepreneurial success index, begin by looking at the results of the Entrepreneurial Aptitude Test Summary Sheet in Appendix A. Compute the three components of the entrepreneurial success equation by using the Entrepreneurial Aptitude Test Summary Sheet for:

OUTER PSE ADAPTABILITY FACTOR

Use bold box IA
Example: If box IA had 12
Outer PSE Adaptability Factor = 12
Your Outer PSE Adaptability Factor =_____

ENTREPRENEURIAL PERSONALITY TRAITS FACTOR

Add bold boxes IIA, IIIA, IVB, and VB
Example: If box IIA had 13
box IIIA had 13
box IVB had 13
and box VB had 13
Entrepreneurial Personality Traits Factor = 52
Your Entrepreneurial Personality Factor =_____

OPERATIONAL TRAITS FACTOR

Add bold boxes VIA, VIIB, and VIIIA
Example: If box VIA had 12
box VIIB had 12
and box VIIIA had 12
Operational Traits Factor = 36
Your Operational Traits Factor = _____

78

EXAMPLE: Outer PSE Adaptability Factor 12
+ Entrepreneurial Personality Traits Factor 52
+ Operational Traits Factor 36
Entrepreneurial Index = 100
Your Entrepreneurial Success Index = _____

The possible scores for the entrepreneurial success index
range from zero to 100. *However, the average score for
this test is 56.* The following table will give you an idea of
your likelihood to be successful in the entrepreneurial arena:

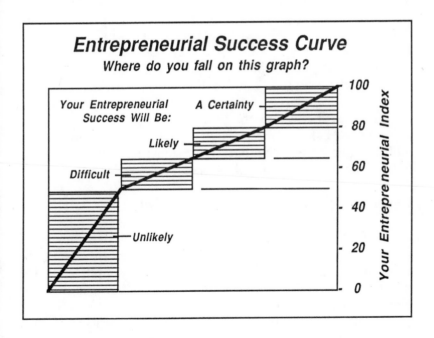

If Your Entrepreneurial Index **Lies Between**	On Your Present Course - **Entrepreneurial Success**
100 - 80	Is a virtual certainty
79 - 65	Is likely
64 - 50	Is difficult without new skills
49 - 0	Is unlikely without new skills

Where your entrepreneurial success index lies in the table above will give you a good idea of your resources in the entrepreneurial arena. If you had a low score in the Entrepreneurial Aptitude Test, there are ways that you can improve your potential for business success. Consider the scores of all three factors of the Entrepreneurial Success equation: Outer PSE Adaptability (12 points possible), Personality Traits (52 points possible), and Operational Traits, which was designed to include discipline but excludes the idea section of the test (36 points possible). If any of your scores are particularly low, place special emphasis on these. Also be aware of differences between **your** psychological type or operational style and the *classic entrepreneur's*. Differences in these areas indicate specific personality or operational traits that may need to be emphasized in your entrepreneurial activities.

Improving your outer PSE adaptability

An area that you can quickly improve is your outer PSE adaptability. This area is usually a weakness in introverted individuals. In doing this you must focus on improving the interface between your sphere and the outside world. A large part of this improvement must center on the area of effective communications. There are two levels to consider in effectively communicating. The basic level includes communicating within your sphere. The other level deals with the ability to communicate outside your personal sphere of equilibrium. Communication outside of your sphere, in an effective manner, is by far the more important. It is this type of communication that is usually needed to begin a new venture.

What can you do to improve your communication link with the outside world? Becoming more familiar with it will help. One way is to execute well-thought-out exercises that will enable you to leave your PSE gradually and in a controlled fashion. This may appear trivial but taking that first small step to solving a problem is often the most important. In other words, try to acclimate yourself to dealing with your outer sphere by initially exposing yourself to small, regular *doses* of your outer PSE. For example, if in the start-up period of your business you must meet with several individuals in positions of authority, try to schedule the meetings at well spaced time intervals. This will reduce the pressure on you by giving you the opportunity to be well prepared for each meeting. You will also find that each subsequent meeting will become a bit easier. In other words, it will become easier to make other excursions from your sphere, thus impacting your plans in an even more positive manner - *success breeds success.*

Influencing your personality traits

If your psychological type differs significantly from that of the *classic entrepreneur* (ENTP), as we mentioned before, there is little that you can do to change your psychological type. However, there are ways to influence your personality, to enhance your *entrepreneurial effectiveness.* These were discussed earlier and include: teaming with others that have the skills that you lack, using advisors and simply being aware of your operational style and making an effort to suitably modify your typical behavior in critical situations. You will never significantly change how you think, but being **aware** of the manner in which you prefer to operate may enable you to modify it a bit.

Improving your operational traits

If your Entrepreneurial Aptitude Test score was low in the operational traits area, improving it is also possible. This area is affected by both your experiences and your personality traits. Examine the Entrepreneurial Aptitude Test Summary Sheet to see if perhaps one or two of the operational traits (idea, strategy, plan or implementation) are unusually low. Typically, strategy and planning are areas that feeling individuals have difficulty with. By definition, they prefer to function in a feeling manner as opposed to a factual or logical manner. They should be particularly aware of these areas. Also, focusing on and trying to improve the idea, strategy and planning areas can be facilitated through objective help. You can get help with the idea or concept, formulating the strategy and the detailed plan but you're alone when it comes to implementing. Implementing can only come from within, you must do the implementing.

Poor implementation can often be traced to poor discipline. Discipline is essential to accomplishing anything. If you are not well disciplined, generally speaking, there is little that you can do in any particular project to improve it. This is so since, as was mentioned before, discipline is related to your value system, and you can't easily change your value system. However, since discipline is related to your value system, if for example, starting your own business represents something that you really want to <u>do</u> - something you value, you will naturally have the discipline to accomplish this goal - even if you are <u>generally</u> not well disciplined.

It should be emphasized that your results in the Entrepreneurial Success Equation are intended to serve as more than a measure of your entrepreneurial ability. The Entrepreneurial Aptitude Test and Equation are intended to be used as tools to help you prepare for the entrepreneurial arena - to start your company. This test will help you understand what is required of you, your personality traits that will help you, your personality traits that may inhibit you and your operational traits that are strengths and weaknesses. Having this information will greatly enhance your probability for finding business success. Further, keeping your personal psychological and operational profiles in the *back of your mind* during your day-to-day start-up activities of your new business, will help you to make the necessary corrections to your style of operating to insure success.

You now have a better understanding of yourself and are, therefore, better able to do what you have always wanted to do - start your own business. Perhaps you simply want to improve upon the business that you have already begun or to find success in some other area. All that is left, is for you to use this information in a plan of action.

Have you formulated your strategy and outlined a plan? Consider the advantages and disadvantages of your various options and select the option with the most merit. After your strategy is developed, begin formulating your plan. There are a number of well established approaches to planning. The one that we favor, because its concepts closely parallel some of the logic of this book, is "Open Systems Planning." Open Systems Planning is well recognized and used by many successful corporations. The philosophy of this approach is basically that the plan being formulated must take into account not only the unit for which the plan is being formulated (your business) but its environment as well. In other words, a plan for a company, organization or individual must be formulated in the context of its environment or it simply won't work. This approach is similar to that of the PSE model which stresses that unless you consider and deal with your external environment, it is unlikely that you will become successful.

The first step in your planning exercise is to identify your mission. You must know what you would like to achieve. You can get advice in this area, especially with identifying various options, but you must make the final decision - it must come from within. The next step is to outline the various skills, abilities, knowledge and any other resources that are necessary to achieve your mission. How do these compare to the inventory or resources that you identified as being present in your sphere? You may also want to include a number of fundamental supporting "milestones" along the path that are essential to the success of your overall business plan.

To insure that your plan is in fact feasible, that is, it can be accomplished, "reality testing" in the external environment should be conducted. Have qualified individuals reviewed and commented on your plan? Your plan must not only make sense from a personal point of view, but it must mesh with your external environment - otherwise it will fail.

The Open Systems Planning theory suggests that your plan must permit you to act on (transform) information gathered from your external environment to your benefit. In other words you should take advantage of information and resources outside of your sphere as well as within. A sound plan will enable you to promote effective *action* in the area of accomplishing your objectives rather than to be forced into *reaction* to everyday circumstances.

To accomplish your plan, you have only the resources in your sphere at your immediate disposal. Let's begin with accepting the fact that you can't change your background. In a sense, you are what you are - your sphere has in it only what you have been exposed to. You are, however, certainly capable of making better use of your immediate resources and those outside of your sphere.

CHAPTER VIII

The Role Of Entrepreneurship In Corporations

What is the role of entrepreneurship, in large corporations? Does it have a role? We have already discussed some of the differences between executives of large corporations and entrepreneurs. One key difference in attitude is that executives are usually more rigid in their operating styles. They have difficulty in changing direction after a mission has been endorsed by their staff and begun. Entrepreneurs, on the other hand, typically exhibit more flexibility and are more likely to adopt new philosophies and direction for a project after it is already under way - both styles have their advantages. Corporate America, however, has been recognizing the advantages of promoting the entrepreneurial spirit within its industries. Executives are attempting to develop working entrepreneurial programs within their companies - notably, in the traditional heavy industries such as: steel, aluminum, glass, and others. Many corporate executives have concluded that the often prolific entrepreneurial process should be applicable within corporate structures as well as in the private sector. In fact, the author proposes that the same criteria, guidelines, and many of the limitations that govern individual entrepreneurial success, apply in the management of large corporations as well.

Obviously, one way to promote the entrepreneurial spirit within a corporatate structure is to introduce a level of decentralization. This can be accomplished by *spinning-off* unique projects for development by the individuals that originally championed them. Some companies are also providing more creative environments and incentives to key management individuals. Founders of these projects assume the role of an entrepreneur bridging the interface between their corporation and the external environment and marketplace. Like other entrepreneurs, they must use their personal abilities, skills and contacts to promote their projects. It should be emphasized, however, that usually, the *corporate entrepreneur* has the distinct advantage of more in-depth resources at his or her disposal .

A corporation represents the management, employees, assets, liabilities, and anything and everything else with which the organization is involved. Corporations exist in environments similar to those of individuals. That is, they have friends, contacts, responsibilities, assets, goals, etc. It is therefore reasonable to assume that they operate in a **corporate sphere of equilibrium** similar to that of an individual.

To infer that companies exist in a sphere of equilibrium is simply a natural extension of the personal sphere of equilibrium model for individuals. As you might expect, however, spheres of equilibrium of corporations are usually much broader and perhaps more dynamic than personal spheres.

When considering the ways corporations function or prefer to operate, they also may be thought of as having a psychological type. The *effective psychological type of a corporation* is probably a _mix_ of the psychological types of the key upper management personnel who actually make the decisions, choose the direction, and implement the daily management of the company. In other words, corporations tend to operate in a preferred style compatible with their effective psychological type.

Corporations, as do individuals, look to the future by setting goals. These goals may deal with issues such as targeting specific new markets, increasing profit margins, promoting internal growth, influencing growth by acquisition, etc. In fact, goal setting is a basic element in the management style of many corporations. For quite some time it has been common for corporations to adopt a management style called "Management by Objectives", a goal-oriented management system. The management of a company is responsible for setting the overall goals, and each manager (together with his supervisor) sets his or her specific objectives so as to support the overall business plan. Goals also tend to provide guidance for a company. Goals are usually included as part of strategic and operating plans, sometimes called business plans. If no such plans exist, the direction of the corporation will be left to chance. This reasoning is similar to the setting of goals and the planning of one's own life and of course one's own company or business.

How then does a corporation grow, become more profitable, and find success? The same way an individual does - by expending energy outside its sphere of equilibrium. Based on this thought, it is possible to postulate a management approach that would encourage and facilitate corporate success. This approach would emphasize working outside the corporate sphere of equilibrium. It would focus on the mechanism of achieving goals as well as the setting of goals. We have labeled this management approach: **Dynamic Management.** It is similar to the case of the individual focusing on the mechanism of achieving goals as well as the setting of goals.

The distinction between "Management by Objectives" and "Dynamic Management" is important. "Management by Objectives" is a management approach, evolving from a focus on objectives or goals. "Dynamic Management" on the other hand, focuses on the *mechanisms* for accomplishing those objectives or goals. These mechanisms emphasize inducing change by operating outside the corporate sphere of equilibrium. This distinction between "Management by Objectives" and "Dynamic Management" is similar to the distinction between your setting of personal goals and your achieving them by operating outside your personal sphere.

Since the Dynamic Management approach is concerned

with activities intended to institute change rather than keeping the status-quo, it must focus on diverting some energy from activities within the company to areas outside the corporate sphere of equilibrium. The management team then must have a strong interface with the outside world (its external environment). This is not necessarily the case with many corporate management teams. In a sense, the Dynamic Management team must operate in a much broader arena than usual. This management style is less restrictive because it considers external as well as internal resources. By taking advantage of external technology and management resources, significant changes in the direction of the company are facilitated. The brain-storming approach to management may also be an important part of Dynamic Management to identify new options which might otherwise not be considered. Further, the Dynamic Management approach is compatible with Open Systems planning discussed earlier.

A scenario of an Dynamic Management effort in a company might unfold as follows: A strategic or business plan (Open Systems Planning) would be written to define the new areas of interest. An appropriate management team would then be assembled to carry out that plan. Strong emphasis would be placed on determining what information, technology, expertise, and management ability would be needed to fulfill the company's goals or objectives. This exercise would delineate the needed resources within the company and those resources that must be acquired externally. The needed external resources would probably fall into several categories - marketing, technology, engineering, management, etc. It might be decided at this stage to split the management team into task forces, each assigned the mission of gathering pertinent information and solving problems in each of these areas. The manner in which the data is acquired is important, because this information must come from sources outside as well as within the company. Because of this, a highly communicative interface between the internal task forces and the external environment would be essential. This is the key, because the underlying logic of the Dynamic Management approach is to fulfill the company objectives by promoting interaction between the company and its external environment. Various vehicles for information and technology transfer may be used. Examples of these are: external consultants, external advisory board, the acquisition of specific technologies, etc. A principal function of the task forces would be to act as a conduit for this information and technology transfer. After each of the task forces has completed its mission, reports on their findings would be compiled and reviewed by the entire management team.

At this stage the operational plan would be formulated and implemented. Usually, the findings of the task forces would suggest several options to be considered. A contingency plan might also be formulated - in case "all else fails." The implementation of the operational plan would be monitored by the various task force groups to ensure that the various facets of the plan are on target. Assuming the plan was sound and properly implemented, the objectives would be met, thus permitting the company to move forward into new areas.

It is important to emphasize that this management approach focuses on the action taking place at the interface between the corporate sphere of equilibrium and its environment. Therefore, the company is not limited to its own resources, but rather can use external resources as well - this is quite an advantage. Dynamic Management may not be as effective for a company operating in a healthy, status quo posture. Such a company would probably not want to institute dramatic change. On the other hand, this management style is suitable for a young dynamic company looking for growth, change in direction, or the solving of serious internal problems.

The comparison between Dynamic Management and more traditional management approaches is somewhat analogous to the comparison between the style of operations of the entrepreneur as compared to the business executive. The entrepreneur typically has a more open style of gathering

89

information, uses every available contact possible and is more flexible, action-oriented and likely to change direction if necessary. This style of operation mirrors the Dynamic Management System which promotes flexibility and the using of all resources available, wherever they may be. On the other hand, the executive is more decisive, inflexible and goal-oriented, a style more compatible with more traditional management styles like management by objectives. **The Dynamic Management System proposed here is a strong candidate for adoption by companies attempting to build new business bases by introducing more entrepreneurial programs into their corporate structures.**

CHAPTER IX

Starting A Business From Scratch

Much of this book has been devoted to the philosophy and mechanism of changing your life, with particular emphasis on starting your own business. It is therefore fitting that the final chapter of this book deal with the more pragmatic mechanism and details of starting a company. Most people, if not all, at one time or other, have entertained the idea of working for themselves. Almost everybody is intrigued by the thought of being his or her own boss. In spite of this, relatively small numbers of people actually work for themselves. After reading this book, the reason for this should be more apparent to the reader. Moving into an entrepreneurial venture requires changing one's life habits, moving from one's sphere - it's also true that specific strengths and skills give one an advantage. Careful self-evaluation is necessary to determine your personal profile as it relates to being successful in business. The final step is usually the acquisition of the skills and strengths that are necessary, but are lacking within your sphere - these must be acquired elsewhere. In no uncertain terms, life-changing processes are complex. This is basically the reason that many people never change their lives significantly. That change they would like to make, but never do, may be starting their own company. This is primarily why The *Fingerprint of the Entrepreneur* was written, to elucidate and make the reader aware of this

91

life-controlling reasoning. Also, the reader is now in a position to take advantage of it.

To be sure however, there are specific pragmatic steps to beginning any business: the more traditionally thought of stepping stones to starting a business. When beginning any business it is a good idea to prepare a business plan, often called a strategic plan. This plan should include the overall strategy to be used in the set-up and operation of your new business. It will also include a financial plan, marketing plan and a plan of action. The plan of action insures that everything will get done. Business plans range from complex to very simple. You should compile and write a plan that at least briefly addresses the above elements. An outline to help you prepare your business plan is included in Appendix C (complete this first). Your business plan will act as the basis for formulating your action plan. In this chapter, we will discuss the steps of a typical action plan in a systematic manner. This will provide you with a detailed outline from which you can prepare your own plan of action for your business. The following is a typical business start-up action plan outline:

1. List the businesses in which you have an interest

This list may include only one type of business or it may include several. In choosing your business, there are certain considerations that are important. Most businesses can be roughly classified into three types:

- Service

- Manufacturing

- Sales

There are subtle but important differences in these. Service companies, for example, usually require the smallest initial capital outlay. Since the product provided is a service, no inventory is required. This is not the case with manufacturing and sales businesses, usually an inventory is required. Also, with service and sales companies, relatively little equipment is required, this is not the case in manufacturing. Other considerations are also important and depend upon the type of company you choose, for example: location, type of building, size, number of employees, etc.

Perhaps the most important consideration in choosing a business is the marketplace. You must determine if there is a logical niche in the marketplace for your service or product and also, how strong your potential competition will be. Most successful companies manage to identify a need in the marketplace and they fill that need effectively. Remember, it is much more difficult to create a need than to fill an existing one. In the final analysis, however, your choice in starting a business should also reflect your personal interests - a company that you would enjoy running. After all, this is one of the rewards associated with going into business for yourself.

2. Establish the manner of acquiring your business

There are two basic ways to acquire a business:

• Start a new business from scratch

• Acquire an existing business

Both of the above options have advantages and disadvantages. One of the major advantages of starting a business from the conceptual stage is that it is usually less expensive than acquiring a similar business. Although there are start-up costs associated with beginning any new business, the cost to acquire a similar existing business is usually substantially higher because of the goodwill factor. Goodwill is the value placed on an ongoing business that allows for the established business potential already developed. Another way to look at this is: When you acquire an existing company, you are buying the ability to conduct business with an established market the

93

very first day you purchase the company. Acquiring an existing company or starting one from scratch represents a trade-off between shortening the time to generate a profit and increased initial capital outlay. When you acquire a company, in theory, you are paying for the time and effort that it would take to build that company.

3. Choose a name for your company

Considerable thought and care should be taken in picking a good name for your new business. As much as is possible, your company name should reflect your unique service or product in a concise easily remembered way. Considerable thought and psychology are involved with choosing a business name. Everybody has an idea on this subject. Do the best you can - it is definitely worth the effort.

4. Fictitious name search

If you choose to operate a business under a name other than your own, your proposed name must be registered after a fictitious name search is conducted. The search is conducted to insure that the proposed name, or a similar one, is not already in use by another business. You can usually personally perform the search in the local county court house records. The name must be subsequently registered and advertised in local newspapers.

5. Inventory your personal skills and strengths

List your personal skills and strengths that will be assets in your new business. For example if you are starting a service company, knowledge, education and experience directly related to the service you will be offering is particularly important. For manufacturing companies, particular knowledge and experience of the product and the details of its manufacturing are important and should be listed. In the sales area, your behavioral traits and characteristics should probably be focused upon along with your knowledge of the product you will be selling and the marketplace. Your interpersonal skills are probably more important in service and sales businesses but play a role in all three types of companies. You must always interact with people. The inventory of resources in your personal sphere (Appendix B), also represents a list of items that should be evaluated and used in starting your new business.

6. Financial net worth statement

Preparing a financial net worth statement will quantify one of the resources that you have at your disposal in starting your new business. Net worth is a measure of your financial resources. Preparing this statement is an important exercise. It establishes the capital that you have available for investment and the proportionate risk that you can afford to take in starting your business. Your net worth statement also gives you some sense of your liquidity, the money quickly available to you. Lending institutions often require a personal net worth statement as part of the requirements for granting business loans.

To prepare a net worth statement, begin by titling and dating the document at the top of the page. List the sum total of your assets on the left of the page and your liabilities on the right. Your net worth is the difference between your total assets and your total liabilities. When listing your assets, be careful not to list the equity value (the part you own) of any particular asset but rather the total value of that asset. This is a common mistake made by individuals when preparing a net worth statement for the first time. The total asset value is balanced by the unpaid debt listed on the liabilities side. Remember, if your net worth is relatively low when attempting to borrow money from a bank or other institution, there are other criteria which may outweigh this factor. An important one is the strength of your business plan for your new venture.

7. Set personal and business goals for six and twelve months

The setting of goals is an important step in the accomplishment of any life-changing objective. Your goals will clearly identify the targets that you are striving for. Once your goals are established, the resources necessary to accomplish them become more apparent. Your goals should be realistic, representing objectives that can be accomplished with a reasonable degree of certainty. Setting of goals that are too ambitious may be the source of wasted time, wasted effort and discouragement. In fact, they may be counter-productive. On the other hand, setting your goals too low, obviously, will not produce results that you are capable of achieving. Seek that happy medium in setting your goals that reflects an objective of significant progress but yet is practically reachable.

8. Discuss your business plans with a lawyer and an accountant

There are a number of options as to the legal form your new business may adopt. For example, you may elect to form a corporation, partnership, limited partnership or simply operate under a sole proprietorship. Which may work best for you and which you choose is dependent upon a number of considerations. This decision is made by weighing the advantages and disadvantages of each form based upon your particular situation. For example, incorporating tends over the long run to reduce personal liability in company matters. However, it has the disadvantage of introducing the possibility of double taxation on funds dispersed to owners of the business. Another example of advantages versus disadvantages is: A limited partnership reduces personal liability to the limited partners, as does a corporation; however, it also relinquishes management control. Sole proprietorships and general partnerships are simpler in structure and are often the best choice for new small businesses. Almost without exception, professional help should be enlisted in helping you select the proper legal form for your new business.

Discussing your business plans with an accountant is equally important. A careful estimate of start-up costs is necessary to insure staying within your initial budget. Also a dependable easy-to-use accounting system should be selected, modified for your particular use, and implemented. Careful financial control and records are necessary to monitor the financial viability of your business. Accounting records are also needed for tax purposes. Professional help is strongly recommended in this area as well, at least in the start-up period of the business. An accounting system can be adopted and set up that requires a minimum of monitoring by a professional accountant - this will help reduce accounting costs.

9. Establish initial funding level required

One of the most common causes of new business failures is undercapitalization. The accountant can also play an important role in determining a conservative estimate of start-up and initial operating costs. An accurate forecast of the costs necessary until the business begins to generate a profit is important. Be sure to include the personal salaries that will be drawn from the business during this development period. A general rule of thumb is that you should have reserves to carry you six to twelve months, depending on the type of business. Be especially conservative when estimating the time period necessary to generate a profit. It is better to err in this estimate with a longer time period than a shorter.

10. Investigate other financing sources

Again, it should be emphasized that the availability of capital is a common problem with many new businesses. If your company is marginally capitalized there are several funding sources that should be considered. Some of these are banks, other lending institutions, independent investors, venture capitalists, and the Small Business Administration. The Small Business Administration is not only a good source for financial help, but also, for information to help with the setting up and operating of your company as well. A critical issue in determining your success in dealing with these lenders is how well you are prepared - the image that you convey. A business plan should be prepared which contains a personal net worth statement, an estimate of your start-up costs, your forecasted revenues and expenses, and a targeted break-even date. This forecast should be well documented with support data from similar businesses. Sections on the business and marketing strategies that are to be employed should also be included. A return on investment one year hence should also be estimated. A good approach in attracting funding for any business venture is to put yourself in the position of the lender. What would make you feel secure if you were making the loan?

11. Review the local, state and federal business laws

There are various permits, licenses and laws that must be acquired or complied with when starting a new business. There are a number of sources for this information. A good way to begin is by looking up the informational telephone numbers for your local, state and federal governments. You should also get advice from an attorney in this matter as well. Some of the general sources for this information are: The Municipal Clerk, the County Clerk, the office of the Secretary of State, and the Small Business Association.

12. Studying your competition

Investigating and becoming familiar with your competition may help you identify that niche in the marketplace that your business can fill. Knowing the strengths and weaknesses of your competitors will also help you compete with them more effectively. Your objective is to capture some predetermined segment of the market.

13. Pick a good location for your business

The location of your business is important. It is naturally more important for some types of businesses than for others. Certain manufacturing businesses, for example, can operate efficiently in many types of locations. In this case, the location is determined, to a great degree, by the rental cost. With other businesses, however (for example, many retail and service companies), the choice of location is of utmost importance. Some of the factors to be considered in locating your business are:

- customer traffic density
- proximity to work force
- proximity to materials, supplies, etc.
- local transportation systems
- location of competitors
- rental costs
- accessibility

14. Choose advertising media

There are a variety of methods to promote your business. The controlling factor in choosing them is their cost effectiveness for your particular situation. Some of your advertising options are: newspaper, radio, television, telephone, tele-marketing, yellow pages, flyers, and word-of-mouth. As a small business becomes established, word-of-mouth can be one of its best forms of advertising. Your reputation will primarily control the effectiveness of this type of promotion. Reputations, however, take time to build and during this early period, some type of advertising will probably be used as part of your marketing strategy. You should establish a budget for advertising. Advertising budgets typically range from a few percent to ten percent of your gross revenues, depending upon the type of business. Your advertising budget should probably be set a little higher in the early stages of your business.

15. Compile a pre-opening day check list

This check list should contain all the necessary advertising, operational and customer interaction elements necessary to insure presenting your companies best possible image on opening day.

16. Set up quarterly goal review procedures

Your progress toward meeting your objectives should be reviewed on a regular basis to insure that your business plan is being fulfilled on schedule and your milestones are being met. Refinement of your plan will most likely be required as you progress. Your periodic reviews will help you to make the necessary modifications to your original plan to insure success.

Implementation of your action plan is your next challenge. The fulfillment of your action plan has associated with it a great reward - the owning of your own business.

Concluding Remarks

We have gone through some sound reasoning describing the manner by which you can accomplish short and long term goals or change the destiny of your life. Remember also our definition of success mentioned in the introduction: *Success has a different meaning to each of us*. Not all of you are interested in becoming entrepreneurs. However, because the concepts presented here are universal, they apply to your personal definition of success - whatever it may be. They hold true for those of you who are not necessarily interested in becoming a *pure entrepreneur* but are interested in business, perhaps in a more casual manner. These concepts will help you to find success in any endeavor by *helping you to change your life.* You can do whatever you wish with your life and this book will help you.

We have examined your personality traits, compared these to typical entrepreneurial traits, and measured your ability to get things done. We have also found that the role psychological traits play may be strongly overshadowed by attitude, desire, and energy. Also, most of you have significant resource reserves in your spheres representing a large untapped potential - you can use this. The fundamental difference between those people who do and those who don't, between those who seem to be able to do everything, and those who have a hard time doing anything, is the way in which they interface with the outside world. It's that simple! Maybe we should rephrase that statement: *If they effectively interface with the outside world.* Successful people aren't necessarily any brighter, better educated, or better equipped. One thing they do, however, is interface with the world more effectively.

We introduced the concept of the personal sphere of equilibrium, explaining that significant, life-changing episodes or events would most likely be initiated outside your sphere and may occur in relatively short time intervals. Those tightly locked within their sphere have less of a chance to be successful. People with the flexibility and courage to move out of their sphere will succeed.

This concept of working outside of your personal sphere of equilibrium may be thought of in terms of risk-taking. Some of you are willing to take risks and others aren't. This is where the entrepreneur has the advantage - he or she is a risk-taker. Generally, the greater the risk, the greater the potential return.

If your definition of success includes entrepreneurship, and you really want to start your own successful business - you can. The following brief outline is to remind you how you will proceed:

- **Take the Entrepreneurial Aptitude Test**
- **Identify and acquire the resources that you need**
- **Manage the risk**
- **Build a solid venture team**

Take the Entrepreneurial Aptitude Test to determine the resources that you have and those that you need. Identify and acquire the missing resources that you lack. Remember, you can't change your personality traits or background, but their are other ways to build strength -- use every available option. If it is appropriate, team with others who have the abilities and traits that you lack. Understand and respect the risk associated with your venture but deal with it head on. Regardless of your skills - your know-how, attitude, and motivation will prevail - also, you now have the knowledge to succeed.

Appendix A

Entrepreneurial Aptitude Test (E Q Test)

Read each question carefully and neatly fill in the appropriate block on the following answer sheet. Use a soft pencil. Do not think too long about any question. Your answer should reflect your initial response to the question.

1. In starting a business, would you be more inclined to
   a. discuss your plans with individuals in a related business field?
   b. discuss your plans with your friends and acquaintances?

2. Do you think you are the kind of person who
   a. is easy to get to know and makes friends quickly?
   b. reveals yourself gradually to others only after you know them well?

3. Do you think that you would be a fairly sympathetic supervisor?
   a. no
   b. yes

4. As a business manager, would you be more
   a. decisive?
   b. careful?

103

5. Would you get more self-satisfaction from
    a. incorporating a new product line into a company?
    b. designing a new product line for a company?

6. Would you
    a. probably consider brainstorming to solve problems in a company?
    b. probably solve problems in a company by more direct methods?

7. Have you established
    a. only a rough plan for accomplishing your goals?
    b. a detailed plan of how to accomplish your goals?

8. Do you
    a. usually finish what you set out to do?
    b. usually have difficulty in following through with things you begin?

9. Have you traveled
    a. fairly extensively?
    b. very little?

10. Would you be more likely to
    a. organize a social function at work?
    b. participate in but not go out of your way to organize the social function at work?

11. In a business dispute, do you think it is more important to
    a. be sure to analyze all the pertinent issues?
    b. be sure to consider the consequences to all parties?

12. Would you describe yourself as
    a. more systematic with a controlled approach?
    b. more spontaneous while keeping open all options?

13. Do you consider yourself
    a. a more practical and down-to-earth person?
    b. a more innovative or idea-person?

14. Would you consider yourself
    a. adept at creative thinking?
    b. uncomfortable with creative thinking?

15. Have you
    a. considered only the overall approach necessary to accomplish your goals?
    b. compared your strengths, weaknesses and resources with those necessary to accomplish your goals?

16. Do you consider yourself to be more of a
    a. disciplined person?
    b. responsible but not an extremely disciplined person?

17. In running your own business, would you naturally tend to
    a. seek out as many contacts as possible to help meet your objectives?
    b. use only well established personal contacts to help meet your objectives?

18. Do you
    a. usually look forward to spending time at social events?
    b. usually think of social events as an activity that you can take or leave?

19. If you were a supervisor firing a subordinate, would you
    a. only slightly take into consideration the impact of this action on his personal life?
    b. strongly consider the impact of this action on his personal life?

20. If you were going on vacation and had a project at work that was almost finished, would you be more comfortable
    a. rushing to finish it before you leave?
    b. not rushing and not finishing it before you leave to insure not making a mistake?

21. In solving a problem, do you
    a. spend most of your time collecting facts and a lesser amount of time deciding what they mean?
    b. spend a lesser amount of time collecting facts and most of your time deciding what they mean?

22. In solving a problem, do you think considering an exhaustive list of options is
    a. beneficial?
    b. a waste of time?

23. Do you
    a. deal with the obstacles in the path of accomplishing your goals as they appear?
    b. identify these obstacles ahead of time?

24. Have you
    a. considered what you can do differently in your life to affect your future?
    b. decided that your present life-style will have little to do with your future?

25. In running your own company, would you tend to
    a. build a team by recruiting others that have the skills that you lack?
    b. choose a strategy that does not require a team effort?

26. Do you consider yourself
    a. usually more outgoing?
    b. usually more reserved?

27. Do you think you are
    a. more inclined to be a fair person that takes into account all of the facts?
    b. more inclined to be a warm and understanding person?

28. If you were painting a room late at night and were tired but could be finished in 45 minutes, would you
    a. be more likely to finish it that night?
    b. be more likely to finish it the next day after you were refreshed?

29. In running a company, do you think it is more important to
    a. be practical?
    b. be intuitive?

30. Would you naturally consider weighing the advantages and disadvantages of a new venture before proceeding?
    a. yes
    b. no

31. Do you usually
    a. fit activities into your schedule?
    b. plan activities in advance?

32. Have you, in your estimation
    a. made significant advances toward accomplishing your goals already?
    b. defined your goals but not made much progress in accomplishing them?

33. Do you
    a. feel reasonably comfortable with risk?
    b. avoid situations involving risk?

34. If you sat next to a stranger in an airplane, would you be more likely
    a. to initiate a conversation?
    b. to have a conversation after it was initiated by the other party?

35. Are you more inclined to be
    a. logical and factual?
    b. sentimental and emotional?

36 If you were involved in an unpleasant situation with your life, would you be more likely to
    a. do something to change the situation even if it may be the wrong move?
    b. not do anything hoping the situation will work itself out?

37. When you make decisions, do you usually
    a. use only the facts?
    b. use the facts along with your intuition or gut feeling?

38. Do you think that
    a. most successful business people plan their destiny?
    b. most successful business people were in the right place at the right time?

39. Have you
    a. focused more on the the initial problems of accomplishing your goals?
    b. outlined all the steps necessary to accomplish your goals?

40. Do you consider yourself more
    a. an expediter?
    b. a procrastinator?

41. If you could have one or the other, would you prefer
    a. autonomy?
    b. security?

42. In a business venture, would you
    a. usually rather work with others?
    b. usually rather work alone?

43. Do you
    a. tend to have a habit of unknowingly ignoring the feelings of others?
    b. usually consider the feelings of others?

44. In running a business, do you think you would usually operate
    a. in a planned, predetermined and controlled manner?
    b. in a flexible, spontaneous manner, ready to make necessary changes?

45. Do you think you are better at
    a. turning ideas into a reality?
    b. originating ideas and letting somebody else execute?

46. Are you more comfortable and better at
    a. figuring out how to solve a problem?
    b. actually solving the problem using a known solution?

47. When you have many tasks to do, do you usually
    a. not list the tasks to be done?
    b. list the tasks to be done?

48. Do you
    a. usually finish things on time even though it may mean rushing a bit?
    b. find that you would rather be late and be sure the job is done perfectly?

49. Would you be more likely to
    a. pursue a business venture with higher risk and greater potential return?
    b. pursue a business venture with lower risk and smaller potential return?

50. Do you
    a. usually think of how to phrase your speech while speaking?
    b. usually think of exactly what you are going to say before you speak?

51. As a supervisor, would you
    a. tend to forget to give recognition to others?
    b. almost always make a special effort to give recognition to others?

52. Do you
    a. tend to finish things or look for resolution on issues?
    b. tend to leave things unfinished or up in the air?

53. Have you ever had an idea that you thought might be the basis for an invention?
    a. no
    b. yes

54. When entering into a new venture, do you think you are better at
    a. considering various options of how to proceed?
    b. actually getting on with the venture?

55. Do you consider yourself more
    a. disorganized?
    b. systematic?

56. Do you
    a. think it helps you to complete things if you set your own deadlines?
    b. not like setting deadlines even imposed by yourself?

57. If you had an important business decision to make, would you probably
    a. ask the advice of others in that field of expertise?
    b. make the decision alone?

58. As a business manager, would you be
    a. more action oriented?
    b. more likely to reflect on matters before acting?

59. In a position of authority, do you think you would
    a. usually not let arguments upset you?
    b. usually get upset by arguments?

60. Do you
    a. usually like to finish one project before starting another?
    b. feel comfortable becoming involved in many projects simultaneously?

61. Would you describe yourself more as
    a. a person that lives life focussing more on the present?
    b. a person that lives life in anticipation constantly looking toward the future?

62. Do you think you have more of a knack for
    a. solving problems?
    b. applying their solutions?

63. When you have a project to do, are you more likely to
    a. let things fall into place as you go along?
    b. plan it in detail?

64. Do you
    a. like to get things done on time?
    b. usually put things off until the last minute?

65. Would you be more likely to
    a. take a job with no base salary but potentially high commission?
    b. take a similar job with a modest guaranteed base salary and a potentially modest commission?

66. Would your friends describe you as
    a. more impulsive?
    b. more reluctant to try something until you understand it completely?

67. Do you
    a. usually consider mainly the facts when making a key decision?
    b. usually consider the facts and the feelings of others when making a key decision?

68. Are you
    a. not easily swayed from your opinion?
    b. more willing to listen open-mindedly to others?

69. When doing a task, do you
    a. do it the way you know will be acceptable?
    b. often try to find a new and better way to do it?

70. Do you consider yourself better at
    a. formulating strategy?
    b. proceeding with the plan after the strategy has been set?

71. Which describes you better
    a. a person who waits until the last minute?
    b. a person who plans ahead?

72. If you have a number of things to do at one time, do you
    a. initially consider them all and then proceed?
    b. consider and do them one at a time?

73. Would you get more self-satisfaction
    a. from a personal successful venture?
    b. as a successful corporate executive?

74. Do you
    a. almost always offer your opinion on an issue?
    b. only offer your opinion on an issue if it involves you?

75. Do you consider yourself more of a
    a. reasoning person and therefore, interested in mainly the facts?
    b. compassionate person interested in the facts to some degree but in the personalities involved as well?

76. In running your own company, would you be likely to
    a. make key decisions as soon as possible?
    b. keep as many options open in key decision situations as long as possible?

77. Would you get more self-satisfaction from
    a. building a new device for manufacturing in your company?
    b. designing a new device for manufacturing in your company?

78. When thinking of a complex problem, do you usually
    a. consider the over-all interpretation of the problem?
    b. focus on one or two facets of the problem?

79. Which describes you better?
    a. a person who usually ignores detail
    b. a person who usually pays attention to detail

80. Do you
    a. make it a habit to set target completion dates of things you would like to do but cannot find time for?
    b. know that you will eventually do the things you would like to do but cannot find time for?

81. Are you more likely to
    a. do whatever it takes to finish a job that you began?
    b. apply only a reasonable amount of effort to finish a job?

82. Do you
    a. usually find yourself acting first and thinking later - sometimes after making a mistake because of your quick action?
    b. usually think things out in detail before acting - sometimes waiting too long to be effective?

83. Do you consider yourself to be
    a. more inclined to be fair, regardless of the outcome?
    b. more inclined to be sympathetic, even if you have to bend the facts a bit?

84. In running your own business, do you think you would be more
    a. decisive?
    b. flexible?

85. In running your own business, do you think you would be more
    a. practical?
    b. imaginative?

86. Do you usually focus more on
    a. an overview of a critical situation?
    b. the details of a critical situation?

87. Are you
    a. usually impatient with planning?
    b. usually comfortable with planning?

88. In general, would you describe yourself as more
    a. motivated?
    b. unmotivated?

89. Do you consider yourself to be more
    a. charming?
    b. direct?

90. In your leisure moments, do you usually prefer
    a. people to help you unwind?
    b. solitude?

91. Do you consider yourself to be a warm and sensitive person?
    a. no
    b. yes

92. Do you tend to leave issues undecided?
    a. no
    b. yes

93. Would you be more likely to run your own business
    a. in a proven and tried manner?
    b. in an innovative, progressive and new-approach manner?

94. Do you think you are better at
    a. formulating strategy?
    b. carrying strategy through?

95. Do you usually
    a. act before you think things out?
    b. think things out before you act?

96. Are you more likely to
    a. keep your New Year's resolutions?
    b. not keep your New Year's resolutions?

97. Do you consider yourself a person with
    a. quite a bit of social charm?
    b. about average social charm?

98. As a business manager, do you think you would be more
    a. callous?
    b. compassionate?

99. Do you often become involved in many projects at once and have difficulty finishing them?
    a. no
    b. yes

100. Do you often become impatient with details and tend to skim over them?
    a. no
    b. yes

If you are interested in a more in-depth and comprehensive evaluation of your E Q test which focuses on your personal entrepreneurial profile, including suggestions that will help you in your entrepreneurial endeavors, do the following:

Send your original answer sheet (make a copy of it first for your own use) with $4.95 for processing, evaluation, tax and postage to:

Laserlight Publishing
Suite 104-337
6992 El Camino Real
Rancho La Costa, CA 92009

Answer Sheet
Entrepreneurial Aptitude Test (E Q Test)

Use a soft pencil - darken selected boxes completely

(This answer sheet may be copied and submitted by your friends)

↖ *Add Totals across the page* ⟶ ↗

	1	9	17	25	33	41	49	57	65	73	81	89		TOTALS	
a	□	□	□	□	□	□	□	□	□	□	□	□		a	I
b	□	□	□	□	□	□	□	□	□	□	□	□		b	

	2	10	18	26	34	42	50	58	66	74	82	90	97		
a	□	□	□	□	□	□	□	□	□	□	□	□	□	a	II
b	□	□	□	□	□	□	□	□	□	□	□	□	□	b	

	3	11	19	27	35	43	51	59	67	75	83	91	98		
a	□	□	□	□	□	□	□	□	□	□	□	□	□	a	III
b	□	□	□	□	□	□	□	□	□	□	□	□	□	b	

	4	12	20	28	36	44	52	60	68	76	84	92	99		
a	□	□	□	□	□	□	□	□	□	□	□	□	□	a	IV
b	□	□	□	□	□	□	□	□	□	□	□	□	□	b	

	5	13	21	29	37	45	53	61	69	77	85	93	100		
a	□	□	□	□	□	□	□	□	□	□	□	□	□	a	V
b	□	□	□	□	□	□	□	□	□	□	□	□	□	b	

	6	14	22	30	38	46	54	62	70	78	86	94		
a	□	□	□	□	□	□	□	□	□	□	□	□	a	VI
b	□	□	□	□	□	□	□	□	□	□	□	□	b	

	7	15	23	31	39	47	55	63	71	79	87	95		
a	□	□	□	□	□	□	□	□	□	□	□	□	a	VII
b	□	□	□	□	□	□	□	□	□	□	□	□	b	

	8	16	24	32	40	48	56	64	72	80	88	96		
a	□	□	□	□	□	□	□	□	□	□	□	□	a	VIII
b	□	□	□	□	□	□	□	□	□	□	□	□	b	

Transfer these Total boxes: ⟶
to the equivalent boxes on the following Summary Sheet

Summary Sheet
Entrepreneurial Aptitude Test (E Q Test)

I. TOTAL A [ ] ←OUTER PSE ADAPTABILITY TOTAL B [ ] — PSE
(strength) (weakness)

II. E [ ] ←EXTROVERTED / INTROVERTED→ [ ] I

III. T [ ] ←THINKING / FEELING→ [ ] F

IV. J [ ] ←JUDGING / PERCEIVING→ [ ] P

Personality Traits

V. S [ ] ←SENSORY INTUITVE→ [ ] N
V. C [ ] Conformer IDEA Originator→ [ ] O
(weakness) (strength)

VI. M [ ] Mastermind ←STRATEGY Detailer [ ] D
(strength) (weakness)

VII. H [ ] Haphazard PLANNING Layout→ [ ] L
(weakness) (strength)

VIII. G [ ] Go-getter ←IMPLEMENTATION Vacillator [ ] V
(strength) (weakness)

Operational Traits

- Fill in the total A and B blocks using the Total boxes at the bottom of the previous answer sheet.
- Psychological type is represented by the larger numbers for each of the sections: II,III,IV and V.
- Operational style is represented by the larger numbers for each of the sections: V,VI,VII and VIII.

Appendix B

Your Personal Resource Inventory

Education
        Formal education
        Informal education
        Trade or craft expertise
        Experience
        Skills
        Talents
        Languages
        Knowledge

Personal Contacts Network
        Acquaintances
        Family
        Friends
        Colleagues
        Tradespeople
        Investors
        Professional contacts
        New business contacts
        Advisors
        Bankers
        Attorneys
        Accountant

Helpful Personal Traits
Diligent
Disciplined
Good with people
Flexible
Risk taker
Idea person
Good with details
Extroverted
Logical thinker
Good strategist
Innovative
Patience
Optimism
Charming

Material Resources
Real estate
Computers
Equipment
Vehicles
Tools
Furniture

Financial Resources
Investors
Credit
Net worth statement (Appendix C)

Motivation and Enthusiasm
Energy
Time
Willingness
Attitude
Enthusiasm

Appendix C

Your Business Plan Outline

Your business plan should contain several sections covering the specific areas outlined in this appendix. These areas: 1) Basic Business Background and Philosophy, 2) Financial Considerations, 3) Strategy, 4) Marketing Plan and 5) Action Plan, include the basic elements of a sound business plan. This outline is intended to include pertinent information for your new venture along with your own thoughts and ideas to amplify the document. From this outline, your business plan may easily be written. Your plan need not be lengthy or complex but should contain this basic information.

1) Background and Overall Business Philosophy and Strategy - This section of the plan will briefly describe the business that you will be starting, including: background information, how it will operate, how and why it will be successful, and the overall methods that you will use to begin and operate it profitably.

2) Financial Considerations - This plan will include an estimate of start-up expenses, forecast of revenues and expenses (including salaries) until an estimated break-even date. The financial forecast of revenues, expenses and profit should be completed for the first year. Also, an estimate of return on investment should be included.

3) Strategy - The strategic plan will basically outline the overall mission of your business. It will describe the exact nature of the business that you are undertaking, your objectives and how you intend to reach those objectives. The focus of the strategic plan will be on how your mission will be accomplished. It will also attempt to describe the exact market that your business will address and how you will capture a significant portion of that market.

4) Marketing Plan - This area will contain a detailed marketing strategy and a marketing budget. The marketing plan will help support the objectives defined in the previous strategy area. This section will also include an outline of the advertising methodologies that you will use in your marketing approach.

5) Action Plan - This plan basically contains your business implementation plan described in the sixteen steps of chapter IX, "Starting A Business From Scratch." Use that chapter as your outline and list any specific thoughts or ideas that you may have to help you carry out your plan.

Activation Energy - the initial relatively small amount of energy needed to make a process or event begin.

Classic Entrepreneur - a fictitious model entrepreneur having all the qualities of a *perfect* business person.

Comfort Zone - the personal sphere of equilibrium in which individuals operate comfortably.

Corporate Sphere of Equilibrium - the operational sphere of a company that is the counterpart of the personal sphere.

Dynamic Management - a management style based upon utilizing resources outside of the corporate sphere as well as within.

ENTP Type - the psychological type of the *ideal* entrepreneur.

Entrepreneur - one who organizes, manages and assumes the risk of a business or enterprise.

Entrepreneurial Aptitude Test - a test designed by the authors to measure one's aptitude in the entrepreneurial arena.

Entrepreneurial Success Index - an index on a scale from 0 to 100 which measures entrepreneurial ability.

E Q Test - Entrepreneurial Aptitude Test that was developed in the research for this book.

Equilibrium Principle - a principle that states: an isolated system will eventually gravitate toward an equilibrium or stabilized condition unless it is acted upon by external forces.

Fingerprint of the Entrepreneur - the entrepreneurial profile of the ideal or *classic* entrepreneur.

Open Systems Planning - a style of operation for companies that acknowledges that they exist in an external environment.

Operational Style - the style an individual prefers to use in the accomplishment steps: idea, strategy, planning, and doing.

Operational Style Matrix - an original matrix which outlines the traits of the sixteen operational styles.

Operational Traits Factor - the contribution to the entrepreneurial success index resulting from operational style.

Outer PSE Adaptability - the ease with which one operates out of his or her personal sphere of equilibrium.

Outer PSE Adaptability Factor - the contribution to the entrepreneurial success index resulting from one's ability to work outside of his or her personal sphere of equilibrium.

Personality Traits Factor - the contribution to the entrepreneurial success index resulting from personality traits.

Personal Sphere of Equilibrium - the equilibrium sphere of interaction of friends, contacts, activities, events, and needs that surrounds each of us in our day-to day lives.

Preferred Preferences - the psychological preferences from the four typing pairs with which a person feels comfortable.

PSE - see Personal Sphere of Equilibrium.

Psychological Types Matrix - an original matrix which outlines the traits of the sixteen psychological types.

Psychological Typing - a psychological process to measure the personality type of an individual - there are sixteen types.

Index

A FINAL THOUGHT

"The power of knowledge lies in its utilization."

About the Authors

Dr. Edward J. Fasiska is President of Entretec Inc., a California based enterprise specializing in investment banking related to *high technology* products and systems development. Entretec is a technical interface bridging the gap between the pragmatic marketplace and the esoteric research community

Formerly, Dr. Fasiska was Vice President of Mellon Institute, a prominent applied research laboratory focusing on product research in entrepreneurial areas. Prior to that he was the co-founder and President of Materials Consultants and Laboratories, an independently held industrial problem-solving laboratory which was acquired by Carnegie-Mellon University.

Deborah Gay Fasiska is President of Laserlight Publishing. Laserlight features a number of original publications including a monthly business-oriented newsletter in the San Diego area. She is also the former president of Architectual Greetings, an innovative art applications company that utilized the mix of art and technology to create its final products. Deborah is an artist, publisher and above all, an entrepreneur.

Dr. and Mrs. Fasiska are a husband and wife team who have a keen focus on the entrepreneurial arena with emphasis on small business *start-ups*. They are an excellent example of *opposites* joining forces to form a successful complementary team in business. They are particularly interested in the related area of how people initiate life-changing actions.

For additional copies of this book:

Send $11.95 plus $2.00 postage and handling
to Laserlight Publishing (address below).   For
orders of 10-20 books, a 10% discount, and for
orders of over 20 books, a 15% discount will be
given.